MW01673303

THE SUMMER OF THE GREAT-GRANDMOTHER

Also by Madeleine L'Engle

A Circle of Quiet
The Irrational Season
Ladder of Angels

The Crosswicks Journal
BOOK 2

THE SUMMER OF THE GREAT-GRANDMOTHER

Madeleine L'Engle

The Seabury Press

Copyright © 1974 by Crosswicks, Ltd.

All rights reserved. No part of this book may be reproduced,
stored in a retrieval system, or transmitted, in any
form or by any means, electronic, mechanical, photocopying,
recording, or otherwise, without the written permission of the publisher.

Published 1974 by Farrar, Straus and Giroux
Seabury paperback edition first published 1979

Library of Congress Catalog Card Number: 79-65523
ISBN: 0-86683-945-3 (previously ISBN: 0-8164-2259-1)

Printed in the United States of America
5 4 3 2 1

The Seabury Press
430 Oak Grove
Minneapolis, Minnesota 55403

for the great-grandmother

Contents

I

Summer's Beginning

1

THIS IS THE SUMMER of the great-grandmother, more her summer than any other summer. This is the summer after her ninetieth birthday, the summer of the swift descent.

Once, when I was around twelve, we took a twenty-mile toboggan ride down a Swiss mountainside. The men guiding the toboggan were experienced mountaineers; the accelerating speed was wildly exciting. Mother and I both clutched the sides of the toboggan as we careened around sharply banked curves. The guides could keep it on the hard-packed snow of the path, but they could not stop it in its descent. My mother's plunge into senility reminds me of that toboggan ride.

When I look at the long green and gold days of this summer, the beautiful days are probably more beautiful, and the horrible days more horrible, than in actuality. But there's no denying that it's a summer of extremes.

It might be said with some justification that all our summers are summers of extremes, because when the larger family gathers together we are a group of opinionated, noisily articulate, varied and variable beings. It is fortunate for us all that Crosswicks is a largish, two-hundred-and-some-year-old farmhouse; even so, when four generations' worth of strong-willed people assemble under one roof, the joints of the house seem to creak in an effort to expand. If we all strive toward moderation, it is because we, like the ancient Greeks, are natively immoderate.

This is our fourth four-generation summer. Four Junes ago Mother's namesake and first great-grandchild, Madeleine, was born. We call her Léna, to avoid confusion in this household of Madeleines. Charlotte, the second great-granddaughter, was born fourteen months later. My mother is very proud of being the Great-grandmother.

But she is hardly the gentle little old lady who sits by the fireside and knits. My knowledge of her is limited by my own chronology; I was not around for nearly forty years of her life, and her pre-motherhood existence was exotic and adventurous; in the days before planes she traveled by camel and donkey; she strode casually through a world which is gone and which I will never see except through her eyes. The woman I have experienced only as loving and gentle mother has, for the past several years, been revealing new and demanding facets. When she wants something she makes her desires known in no uncertain terms, and she's not above using her cane as a weapon. She gathers puppies and kittens into her lap; she likes her bourbon before dinner; she's a witty raconteur; and the extraordinary thing about her descent into senility is that there are occasional wild, brilliant flashes which reveal more of my mother-Madeleine than I ever knew when she was simply my mother.

But she is my mother; there is this indisputable, biological fact which blocks my attempts at objectivity. I love her, and the change in her changes me, too.

She was born in the Deep South, spent her married life wandering the globe, in New York and London, and now, in her old age, prefers the more clement weather of North Florida for the winters. But her presence in Crosswicks has always been part of the summers. A friend asked me, "Did you invite your mother to spend the summers with you or did she invite herself?"

I was a little taken aback. "There wasn't ever any question of inviting. We just said, 'When are you coming?' "

"Did you discuss it with Hugh?"

I don't think it ever needed discussion. My mother and my husband have always loved each other—after the very first when Mother wasn't happy about the idea of my marrying an actor. She and Hugh are much alike, in character, in temperament. A stranger would be apt to take Mother and Hugh for mother and son, and me for the in-law. We have always thought of her as part of Crosswicks. She helped make it grow from the dilapidated, unloved old building it was when we first saw it, a quarter of a century ago, to the home it is now. She helped plan my workroom out over the garage, a beautiful study which the children named the Tower. When we lived in Crosswicks year round, while our children were little, she usually spent one of the winter months with us; when we moved back to New York for the school year, this was even more fun for her, because we could go to the theatre, the opera.

I have been so used to having my mother be my friend as well as my mother, to having her be Hugh's friend, that I was surprised at the idea of "inviting" her to spend the summer, and at the implication that this is not the usual way of things.

Perhaps it's not, but having Mother spend the summer in Crosswicks is part of the chronology of the house.

Hugh and I drive to New York, to the airport, to meet her and bring her the hundred miles to Crosswicks. I am shocked when I see her. The plane flight has been harder on her than we had anticipated; the toboggan has continued its descent at an accelerating pace since we saw her at the ninetieth-birthday celebration on April 30. She is confused during the two and a half hours' drive. I hold her hand and try to point out familiar landmarks.

"I don't remember it," she says anxiously. Only occasionally will she see a building, a turn of the road, a special view, and say, "I know this! I've been here before . . . Haven't I?"

We stop at our usual halfway place, the Red Rooster, for lunch, but Mother is too nervous to eat, and we stay only a few minutes, while Hugh and I quickly swallow hamburgers. I continue to hold her hand, to pet her. My emotions are turned off; I do not feel, any more than one feels pain after a deep cut. The body provides its own anesthesia for the first minutes after a wound, and stitches can be put in without novocaine; my feelings are equally numbed. We complete the drive, and I am anxious only to get Mother home, and to bed, in the room which has been hers for a quarter of a century. My thoughts do not project beyond this to the rest of the summer.

I feel very tired, and somehow as though somebody had kicked me.

2

MY MOTHER does not come to Crosswicks in isolated chronology; she comes to a house which, like a river, continuously flows with living. The summer of the great-grandmother began several weeks before her arrival, early in June, while she was still in the South, and her great-granddaughters were still living in England, where their parents, Alan and Josephine, were preparing to break up their home in Lincoln and return to New York. Our younger daughter, Maria, and Peter, with impatience and impetuousness similar to Hugh's and mine a quarter of a century ago, couldn't wait for them. So on the fifth of June Crosswicks was filled with the joy and laughter of a tiny wedding.

The apple blossoms were barely over, the lawn still white from petal-fall. There were a few lingering daffodils in cold and shady corners which keep small drifts of snow long after the rest of the grass has started to turn green. The lilac, purple and white, was in full bloom (the white lilac tree outside Mother's window was a birthday present to her twenty-odd years ago); early daisies and ubiquitous dandelions brightened the big field. Hugh mowed the lawn, trimmed around rocks and trees. Our son,

Bion, just graduated from high school, made countless trips to the dump, fifteen miles away—there's nothing like a wedding to insure a proper housecleaning. And I cooked as though we expected to feed an army instead of a small wedding party.

Maria and I had long, quiet talks. Like her sister Josephine before her, she was apprehensive as the moment approached. I assured her that I had been too. We grew closer in sharing experience.

Peter and I talked, too. He said, "Maria is worried that you don't love me as much as you love Alan." I assured him, "I love you just as much for being Peter as I love Alan for being Alan."

Alan is English, an Anglican priest and theologian. Peter is Jewish, and a theoretical chemist, and that's a superb pair of sons-in-law. A few days ago Peter showed me his most recent published paper and paid me the honor of expecting me to understand his strings of equations, Greek letters, and an occasional English word. He leaves pads of yellow paper lying around on which he has been scrawling a long equation he is trying to think through. Occasionally I will glimpse, off in the corner of my mind, something of what he is driving at, and this happens just often enough to encourage me.

On the day of the wedding, our friend and family godfather, Canon Tom Tallis, drove up to Crosswicks from St. John's Cathedral in New York to perform the wedding ceremony.

In the same large, L-shaped living room where Peter and Maria stood to become man and wife, Hugh and I, newly married, had put on wallpaper, yellow and grey colonial wallpaper which is still on the walls, still beautiful (we are very good wallpaperers). Hugh had spent hours pulling the old bark from the ceiling beams, scrubbing them down; these were the first important acts of making Crosswicks our home. Several years later I rocked Bion in an ancient wooden cradle in front of the fireplace in the long end of the L. The Christmas tree was always in the corner of the L, in front of the heavy door, the "funeral door" which blew in during the blizzard of '88. One Christmas Eve, when our children were small, we all set off for church, leaving the wrapped presents under the tree, and a puppy in the kitchen. When we got home the puppy had got loose and had joyfully unwrapped every single package. Thank-you letters that year ran something like, "Thank you for the lovely present . . ." because nobody had any idea who had sent what.

I have wept in this room; made love in this room, in front of the fire on a cold winter's night; I have waited anxiously for my husband to make a long drive home the length of New England during a terrible wind and snow storm. The house has absorbed and contained much of my married life, of my "grownup" years. The fullness of life in this room filled my heart as we waited for Tallis to begin.

The family wedding party stood in a semicircle—Hugh and me; Peter's mother and two sisters; Bion; plus the cats and dogs, interested in the whole event and ever ready to participate. Tyrrell, Josephine and Alan's dog, half shepherd, half golden retriever, who has been with us for the three years they have been in England, retired under the sofa. The two Irish setter puppies, Faba, who belongs to Tallis, and her sister, Dulcie, who is ours, are less well behaved and I had to order them, firmly, "Sit." Then the words of the wedding ceremony took over and I found that I was close to tears in the presence of these aweful vows my daughter and Peter were taking, the same vows which Hugh and I took, the vows which have held us together through many rough patches.

When I hugged and kissed Maria after the final words were said, I whispered to her, "Now that there has been a wedding here, the house is truly blessed."

That night when everybody had left, except for Hugh and Bion and me, and Hugh and I were ensconced wearily in our four-poster bed, reading, the phone rang. It was Maria and Peter, calling from the International Motel at JFK airport, bubbling with happiness, thanking us—and everybody—for their day; sharing their joy. Josephine and Alan had called from the same place on their wedding night; our travel agent had kept reassuring us that the rooms were soundproof, and it took us a long time to realize that he was referring to the sound of planes.

Laughing, we turned off the lights.

3

AND SO THE SUMMER began with something quite ordinary, two young people getting married. We put the house back into its usual disorder, and I began to concentrate on Mother's arrival. When we went South for the ninetieth-birthday party, we all realized that if Mother was to spend the summer months in Crosswicks as usual, she would have to have a great deal more care than ever before. So we began putting together a bouquet of young girls to tend her, twenty-four hours a day, seven days a week. These girls, friends of our children, are of high school and college age, and this is their summer job. I talked with them informally, trying to tell them what we expected of them, and somehow sensing intuitively that the job was going to be more exacting than any of us anticipated.

The week before Mother's arrival I was to spend teaching at a writers' conference in the Midwest, and I set off, feeling that everything was under control, as much as is humanly possible. How to take care of my mother's summer was my single-minded concern, and I thought I had the summer pretty well organized.

Then, as so often happens when I think that everything is under control, the unexpected struck. My second night at the conference, Hugh phoned and during the conversation told me, trying to make light of it, that he had been feeling some numbness in his feet. He had gone to our doctor, who had made an appointment for him with a neurologist; this could not be arranged for until a week after Mother's arrival.

I hung up, hoping I had kept my voice steady. Only a short while ago a cousin had died of a brain tumor; the first symptom was numbness in the feet. I could not guess whether or not Hugh remembered this. I knew, from the timbre of his voice when we talked again the next night, that he was more concerned than he wanted me to know.

So we moved into the same kind of cold waiting we had known once before, when three-year-old Josephine, during Christmastime, showed all the symptoms of leukemia. The pediatrician, examining her, had talked in obscure medical terminology, and I finally cut him short by saying, "What you mean is that you suspect leukemia—don't you?" "It is a possibility, yes." Once the words were out, he was much more gentle, much more human with us than he had been while he was pussyfooting.

Hugh and I shared our fear mostly in silence. We will never forget the merry little girl's lethargy and pallor, or her quiet stoicism in the hospital lab. Nor will we ever forget the world opening out again when the tests indicated an infection which was already beginning to clear up.

While I was at the writers' conference our sharing had to be on that silent level which precludes words. This was certainly no time to voice my fears to Hugh, or his to me. The only way I could be a wife to him was to affirm silently a courage and endurance I was very uncertain I had.

One of the problems of being a storyteller is the cultivated ability to extrapolate; in every situation all the *what if*s come to me. Often my fears are foolish: if Hugh is ten minutes late in getting home from the theatre he has not necessarily been pushed under a subway train or been stabbed. This time I knew the fear was not the child of my overvivid imagination; it was quite possible that I might have to face my husband's death even before my mother's. My powers of extrapolation were kind enough to slam the door on themselves, at least momentarily.

Still shaken, I went to give a lecture. I talked, as I had originally planned to do, about the precariousness of all life. And I told about walking in midtown New York and having a stone from a nearby half-built skyscraper crash to the sidewalk just behind me. Had I been a fraction of a second slower I would have been killed. And I said that the artist's response to the irrationality of the world is to paint or sing or write, not to impose restrictive rules but to rejoice in pattern and meaning, for there is something in all artists which rejects coincidence and accident. And I went on to say that we must meet the precariousness of the universe without self-pity, and with dignity and courage. It was what I had prepared, several weeks before, to talk about, tying it all in with writing, and our responsibility not to make vain promises of "everything will be all right" to our children. But that day the words were swords which turned to me, to teach me. To challenge me to accept my own words.

Listening to the lecture was one old and close friend who knew of my fears about Hugh, and I was sustained by the necessity not to let her down. What I cannot do for myself, I can sometimes do for somebody else.

That evening in my hotel room where nobody would overhear, I called Pat in Florida. Pat is a doctor, and we have been friends ever since we were in high school. I knew that she would not fob me off with easy answers, and she did not. She did, however, explain calmly and rationally all the things other than a brain tumor which could cause the symptoms. When I hung up I was still fearful, but I knew that there were alternatives.

In any case, one cannot sustain the heights of anguish for too long; this appears to be one of the built-in safety mechanisms of the psyche, and it is a saving grace. My fears for Hugh continued to give me an occasional kick in the pit of the stomach, but mostly they stayed decently in the background, and I was able to get on with the business of daily chores; complete the series of lectures and seminars; return to Crosswicks; prepare for Mother's arrival.

At the moment it is all a chill business because I am living in the cold place of the absence of meaning. And yet I know that if there is anything radically wrong with Hugh I cannot survive it myself, or be a wife and strength and help to him, or be a daughter to my mother, or be a person for my family and friends, unless there is a promise of meaning.

My frail hope is that I was able to lecture while I was impaled on the point of anguish, and that I lectured well—no need for false humility here—and I certainly could not have done it if I truly felt that the universe has no meaning, that there is no point to Hugh's life; or my mother's; or mine.

4

I AM TIRED, and numb. Mother's first two nights in Crosswicks I do not get any sleep, despite my fatigue. She needs more attention during the night than we had expected. The two girls who do night duty are young and completely inexperienced in nursing; Vicki has another year in high school; she was born during the years we lived in Crosswicks year round; it is difficult for me to realize that she is now a young woman, and a very capable young woman. Janet, too, I have known all her life; her father died when she was a baby, and her mother only a summer ago, and I wonder if she does not feel a certain irony in taking care of an old woman who has lived long past normal life expectancy. And I feel that the two girls need help, not physical help, simply my being there, awake and available if they need me.

After the first two wakeful nights it is clear to me how competent they are, and that I must get some rest.

It's a good thing to have all the props pulled out from under us occasionally. It gives us some sense of what is rock under our feet, and what is sand. It stops us from taking anything for granted. It has also taught me a lot about living in the immediate moment. I am somehow managing to live one day, one hour at a time. I have to. Hugh is in Crosswicks for four days, and somehow or other I am able simply to be with him, without projecting into the future. When he goes back to New York he will be going to the neurologist.

Each evening after dinner I walk the dogs down the lane for a few minutes, to catch my breath and regain perspective. The girls prepare the great-grandmother for bed, and we learned the first night that this is done more easily if I am out of the house; if I am there she calls for me, and will not do anything for any of us.

This night, when I return, she has been put to bed, and the larger family—Hugh, Bion, Josephine, the girls, assorted friends and neighbors (Maria and Peter are not back from their honeymoon)—have gathered in the living room to play poker with ancient poker chips. Alan is out in the Tower writing. I'm not a poker player either, so I go in to say good night to Mother and sit with her for a while. Our quiet times together have always been in the morning, over coffee, and at night before bedtime. For a moment, a flash, she is there, is herself, and we laugh at Tyrrell lying on her back, all four legs spread out, tail wagging in this upside-down position. Thomas, the amber cat, is also on his back, lying beside the big dog, rear legs abandoned, forepaws folded prayerfully across his chest. Titus, the yellow puffball kitten, is in Mother's lap, purring.

Then the moment is gone. "Something's wrong,"

my mother says. "I don't know what it is, but something's wrong."

"It's all right, Mother. Nothing is wrong."

"It is, it is. Something's wrong. I want to go home." This has been a constant refrain since her arrival. "I want to go home. I want to go home."

"You *are* home, Mother. You're with your family, with all your children."

"I want to go home."

Yesterday Alan put his arms around me to give me comfort, and said, "Yes, she wants to go home, but she doesn't mean down South."

Her fear touches off an enormous wave of protectiveness in me, and I know no way to keep her terror at bay.

"I want to go home," she repeats.

I sit on the bed beside her, and hold her hand. She fumbles with the other hand for the bell we have rigged up for her. A summer ago she used it sparingly; this summer it seems that the raucous buzz goes off every few minutes. "Mother, you don't need to ring for the girls. I'm right here."

"Where are they?"

"In the living room."

"What are they doing?"

"Playing poker."

She reaches again for the bell.

"Don't call them, Mother. I'm right here." I am obviously a poor substitute. Why am I hurt? This is not my mother who is rejecting me, my mother who was always patient, tolerant, wise.

Then she turns toward me, reaches for me. "I'm scared. I'm scared."

I put my arms around her and hold her. I hold

her as I held my children when they were small and afraid in the night; as, this summer, I hold my grandchildren. I hold her as she, once upon a time and long ago, held me. And I say the same words, the classic, maternal, instinctive words of reassurance. "Don't be afraid. I'm here. It's all right."

"Something's wrong. I'm scared. I'm scared."

I cradle her and repeat, "It's all right."

What's all right? What am I promising her? I'm scared too. I don't know what will happen when Hugh goes to the neurologist. I don't know what's going to happen with my mother this summer. I don't know what the message may be the next time the phone rings. What's all right? How can I say it?

But I do. I hold her close, and kiss her, and murmur, "It's all right, Mother. It's all right."

I mean these words. I do not understand them, but I mean them. Perhaps one day I will find out what I mean. They are implicit in everything I write. I caught a hint of them during that lecture, even as I was cautioning against false promises. They are behind everything, the cooking of meals, walking the dogs, talking with the girls. I may never find out with my intellectual self what I mean, but if I am given enough glimpses perhaps these will add up to enough so that my heart will understand. It does not; not yet.

When Mother is quiet and moving into sleep, I go up to bed. Hugh's and my room is directly over hers. If any architect of theatre or concert hall wants to study acoustics, all he needs to do is come to Crosswicks. A pin dropped at one end of the house can be heard in the other. Bion's room is up in the attic, over ours. If he plays music up there at night, a loudspeaker might as well be concealed in one of the heavy, pineappled posts of our big bed. If I can hear Bion, Mother can hear me. I tiptoe very softly, very carefully.

But it works two ways. Mother can hear any sound from our bedroom. I can also hear her.

The poker players disperse. The household settles down for the night. Cynthia brings me a mug of cocoa with whipped cream *and* a marshmallow. I thank her, saying, "This will put me to sleep."

Cynthia goes into the next room, the nursery, where she sleeps with the two little girls. Her father is one of the canons at the Cathedral in New York, and ever since Léna made my mother a great-grandmother, Cynthia has spent at least part of the summer with us, helping with the children.

I sip the hot cocoa, but it does not put me to sleep. When the rest of the house is quiet, I am still awake, listening for every sound downstairs. I hear Mother turn over, call out. She sounds frightened. I know that I mustn't keep rushing downstairs at her least sound, but I get halfway out of bed, listening, listening. I go out into the hall and stand by the stairs. But there is no further sound. I go back to bed and turn on the light to read and wait for Hugh, who will be reading downstairs for a while in order not to disturb me.

I have found that the German philosophers with their long, cumbersome sentences (never use three words when you can use a hundred and three) are soporific. It is seldom that I can read Kant for more than half an hour without my eyelids drooping.

After a while I turn off the light, but I am still sleeping with one ear open as I did when the children were little, listening for Mother, for the grandbabies, waiting for Hugh.

I sit up in bed: what is that?

It is Bion, climbing up the blue spruce and in through the nursery window so as not to disturb his grandmother by coming in downstairs. He and some of the poker players have been for a midnight swim at Mohawk Pond. He stands in the doorway between nursery and bedroom to talk. I hold my fingers to my lips, not for Cynthia and the babies, who are sound asleep, but for his grandmother.

We planted the blue spruce before he was born. By the time he was a baby, it was big enough for us to use for our outdoor Christmas tree; it could be seen from the main road, a mile downhill, and we always turned it on to welcome Hugh on his way home.The last Christmas we spent at Crosswicks before moving back to New York for the school year, I had to stand on the kitchen step stool, on tiptoe, to fling the string of lights over the top branches. Now the tree is as tall as the house, and Bion can use it for his private, if prickly, stairway.

We whisper for a while, and then he says, "Go to sleep, Mother."

To sleep, perchance to dream.

I love my dreams, and the good ones are so good that they more than compensate for the occasional bad ones, when I wake up and reach out to touch my sleeping husband for comfort. In the past few years my mother has moved slowly into the realm of nightmare; her dreams are frightening; they are controlled and distorted by clogged arteries. She has never slept well, but now she is becoming afraid to sleep.

I hear Bion tramping up the stairs to his attic bedroom. From her crib Charlotte gives a dream cry. There is no sound at all from Mother's room. I must try to sleep.

5

On Monday, Hugh goes down to New York; to the television studio; to the neurologist. All day I am conscious of the telephone. Waiting. Of course it is one day when all kinds of people phone, and although I know that Hugh will not call before late afternoon, my heart jolts with each ring.

The day moves slowly. The children blow dandelion clocks, and their white stars seed the lawn: Hugh will be furious. The sun seems to hold still in the sky. But there are things to do, meals to cook, beds to be made, small duties which push the day along. When the phone rings and I hear Hugh's voice, the timbre strong and vibrant, I know that the news is good. The numbness in the feet is caused by diabetes, is controllable. If I had not been worried about a brain tumor I might have been horribly upset, but we have known about the mild diabetes for over a year; I have already learned how to cook without sugar; all I feel is lightness with the weight of my worst fears removed. I soar like one of the butterflies the children and the puppies love to chase across the big field.

Now that the sword of Damocles has been lifted from our heads, and there's a hope of a future together, I still must neither count on nor fear that future, but live in the present moment, the now. And I must turn my heart fully to Mother, and not let it be torn too much by her infinitely pathetic degeneration. I must not retreat when she is horrid with me, but let it roll off—almost impossible, but I will try. And I must not project into the future and worry about this descent being a long one.

It has not come all at once; there were strong intimations of it more than five years ago, at the time of Josephine and Alan's wedding; and it was definitely accelerated when Mother was given general anesthesia for an intestinal resection when she was eighty-seven. But until this year her mind has been like a summer sky with small white clouds occasionally moving across and blotting out the light of the sun. Each year the sky has become cloudier; there have been fewer periods of sunlight. This summer the sunlight in the sky of my mother's mind, when it shines at all, glimmers through cloud.

❧

Maria and Peter come back from their honeymoon. They are based in Peter's apartment in Philadelphia, where he has been doing post-doctoral work at the University of Pennsylvania, but they come frequently to Crosswicks.

The best part of these slow, long summer days, so different from the rest of the year, is early evening and dinnertime, when the family gathers together after the day's work, the noisy, extreme, diverse people who keep me going. I get dinner started, and then we all sit in the living room for an hour.

The little girls are already fed, bathed, and in their nightclothes; like the puppies and the cats they wander around looking for cuddles and cookies. Léna likes to choose what I am to wear; I enjoy, if there's time, taking a hot, soaky bath, then putting on a long dress or skirt. Léna points to the clothes in my closet: "Dis one, Gan-mad-len."

Gan-mad-len. Her attempt at Grandmadeleine. Charlotte cannot get that far. I am Madden. Neither of the little girls can get her tongue around Great-grandmother, and Léna comes up with Gracchi, which sticks. How to spell it? It sounds something halfway between Grokkie and Grakkie, and Gracchi is as close as I can get to what it sounds like to me. Sometimes Mother is aware enough to be charmed by her new title.

Josephine, too, enjoys a bath and a change of clothes before dinner. Maria wears low-waisted, bell-bottom trousers, which are most becoming to her.

As for the men, Hugh comes in from his vegetable garden wearing frayed shorts made out of an old pair of trousers, and honest sweat. He doesn't call his garden organic, or macrobiotic; he simply gardens the way the first dwellers in Crosswicks gardened, with manure and compost, and no chemical sprays or powders. He brings lettuces and tomatoes and young onions and carrots and peppers and the first small cauliflower into the kitchen and sits down, tired and contented. I make a sauce, and we take the young, raw vegetables into the living room for hors d'oeuvres.

Alan has on a purple, Russian-necked shirt, and comes in from the kitchen bearing freshly made hot clam dip. Peter looks, as usual, like Einstein, hair and all. Bion has been out painting fences all day, and wears jeans and a large quantity of white paint. This is a summer of transition for him, this time between school and college, and it is the first summer since he started high school that he hasn't been away from home for at least a month on some job or other. It is good to have him around, and he has enough painting jobs to keep him busy. He puts a record on the player and drapes six foot four inches of young man over a large chair.

Margie and Cynthia come in with the great-grandmother between them, and settle her on the small sofa. Margie's family lives up the road from us, and one of Margie's older sisters babysat for us when Margie herself was a baby. Margie and Cynthia; Vicki and Janet; Clara, our friend and neighbor from down the road; Bion's friend, Jane, who comes to take the long weekend duty to give the others a break; Polly, from across the lane: it's a multiple job for all of them. They help with the great-grandmother; help with the babies; help with the dishes and housecleaning; everybody pitches in. Cynthia bakes cakes—my cooking falls down when it comes to pastry. Margie cleans and polishes everything and keeps the house full of flowers from the garden, from fields and hedges. This used to be my mother's job; it is something else old age has taken away from her; and from us.

Clara, older, stronger, more experienced than the girls, picks the great-grandmother up nearly every morning and puts her in the bathtub; brushes her still-beautiful hair; dispenses love generously wherever it is needed. The girls bring laughter and music and life. These extraordinary helpers are all ordinary, everyday people, and I couldn't get along without them.

I realize, with a pang, how privileged we are to be able to keep my mother with us. This is how it should be, but what would I do if we lived in a tiny house and did not have the girls and Clara to help? Would I be able to keep her with us, or would I have to put her in a "home"—what an obscene misuse of a word! Homes for the aged, nursing homes, are one of the horrors of our time, but for many people there is no alternative. And even though we have room, and the girls to help us, there are still those who think that my mother should be put away. Put away. Everything in me revolts at the thought. But my belief that we are supposed to share all of life with each other, dying and decay as well as feasting and fun, is being put to the test.

This summer I look at my mother sitting on the small sofa during the hour before dinner and I do not know her; I am looking at a stranger, not because she is old and shrunken and lined, but because the light behind her face is no longer there. Up until a few years ago she was an example of a woman who has experienced life fully, and who grows yearly more beautiful with age. There is little character or loveliness in the face of someone who has avoided suffering, shunned risk, rejected life. It was only when suffering, risk, and life were taken from her by atherosclerosis that Mother's face became an unfamiliar one. (I asked Pat, "What do you call it? Arteriosclerosis? Atherosclerosis?" "Most lay people say arterio, but it's athero.")

A house, like a human being, reflects its experiences. And I do not think that a house can be a happy house if no one has cried in it, if no one has died in it. If this seems contradictory, I can't help it. I rebel against death, yet I know that it is how I respond to death's inevitability that is going to make me less or more fully alive. The house helps me here, because it is a warm and welcoming house, full of life, and yet during the past two hundred years it must have contained many deaths.

Death is the most ordinary thing in the world, and so is birth. Someone is being born at this very moment. Someone is dying. Ordinary, and yet completely extraordinary. The marvel of having my babies is something I will never forget. The feeling of staggering uniqueness I had at the death of my father, the death of several close friends, was very different, but equally acute. Death may be an ordinary, everyday affair, but it is not a statistic. It is something that happens to people.

The most ordinary of deaths is the death of a parent. In this twentieth century we are likely to outlive our mothers and fathers, and more parents are dying senile than ever before. Perhaps this is why old age is respected less. So what I am experiencing this summer (though our doctor tells us that Mother is far from dying) is something I share with a great many other people. And I feel the need to reach out and say, "This is how it is for me. How is it for you?"

6

TALLIS RETURNS from his vacation in England and phones. "How goes it?" He can tell by my voice that the going is rough, and his response is to drive himself right up in his ancient Thunderbird. His own mother died not long ago at ninety-three; he does not need to say anything, nor do I; I know that he knows.

Everybody in Great-grandmamá's retinue enjoys him; long after I have gone to bed they sit around the dining-room table, by candlelight, talking deep into the night.

Sometimes Tallis drives up with our mutual friend, whom we call Anton, because of his resemblance to Chekhov. When Mother first saw Anton with his Chekhovian beard, she announced in a loud clear voice that it was horrible. "I hate it. But you may kiss me anyhow."

Anton, like Tallis, is horrified at the changes in the great-grandmother. Only a summer ago we all sat at the dinner table and laughed while Anton refused to pass the old lady a seventh ear of fresh-picked corn—"I don't know how I ever dared try to stop her," he said. Only a year ago we all literally almost fell off our chairs with laughter when Anton complimented me on dinner and Mother commented, "It ought to be good. I've taught Madeleine everything she knows about cooking." Somehow or other, even through the Depression, Mother almost always managed to have someone in the kitchen. Now, when she is at home in the South, she has an entire retinue, so that she is cooked for and cared for seven days a week.

When Hugh and I were first married and Mother came to visit us, she would offer to help in the kitchen, and she was just about as much help as the grandbabies; and, as with the grandbabies, I had to think up things for her to do. My nanny used to laugh and tell me that when Mother was giving a dinner party, the house would be spick-and-span, and at the last minute in would come Mother with flowers to arrange, leaving leaves and petals on the newly vacuumed rug.

She has always left a trail of flowers behind her. Despite her incorrigible scattering of greenery, she had enormous talent for arranging flowers. When the rather sparse flower garden at Crosswicks had nothing to offer, she could take a collection of weeds from the hedges at the side of the lane, and create a work of art. It wasn't Japanese at all—she was much too lavish—but her arrangements were uniquely hers, and uniquely beautiful. I miss them.

7

THERE IS MUSIC I will never again be able to hear without being plunged into the atmosphere of this summer. It was a year ago that Margie discovered *The Magic Flute.* She played the glockenspiel in the school band, and the charming music of the glock in Mozart's opera delighted her so that she played our records at least daily. The music is more poignant this summer, because she puts it on whenever the great-grandmother is having a bad day. It hurts Margie's lovingness that love is not enough, that it cannot push back the slide into senility.

Bion's new find is Vaughan Williams's *Fantasia on a Theme by Tallis.* This is one of his favorites in the evening before dinner, and Mother still responds to music—it is the last thing to call her forth from the cloud. On the other side of the record are two pieces by Elgar, Introduction and Allegro for String Quartet and Serenade in E minor, which are unfamiliar to Mother (we discovered the Thomas Tallis together, while I was in college), and each evening she tells Bion how beautiful the music is, and asks him, "What is this lovely music, Bion?" "It's Elgar, Grandmother."

During the day the young people play "their"

music. It is understood that this is the time for the Beatles, for Buffalo Springfield, for the Who. Mother does not like such music, and it is good for her to respond to it, to announce loudly how horrible it is. At least it is my theory that it is good, that she should not be isolated by the narrowing of old age. A lot of the time I don't like the music either, but I do not ask to have it turned down. If it is important for Mother to be as full a part as possible of this multi-generation household, it is important for Hugh and me, too.

It is tacitly understood that the evening is reserved for Tallis, Elgar, Bach, Mozart (though not *The Magic Flute;* we've had that with the vacuum cleaner). Sometimes Alan and I will play violin and piano, which, for some reason, Mother has always enjoyed. She is still likely to notice, and remark, when I play a false note; if we are not accurate with tempo, she beats it out on the arm of the little sofa.

Music has always been part of the fabric of her life, so it is not surprising that it is the last thing to reach her. As a young girl, she studied music in Berlin and played well enough to do concert work, which she hated; she went through an agony of anxiety except when playing for friends. During my early childhood, when we lived in New York, my parents used to have an open supper party every Sunday evening, and there were anywhere from half a dozen to two dozen people there. These evenings were centered around the piano—the same piano on which I play in Crosswicks, a piano considerably older than I am, but still with a felicitous tone and a responsive keyboard. Mother used to be able to read piano music the way most of us read a novel, and when friends from the Metropolitan Opera Company were there on Sundays, which was nearly every Sunday during the opera season, Mother would sit down at the piano and read off the score of *Götterdämmerung* or *La Bohème,* while the singers (and sometimes the non-singers) sang. I used to slip out of my room on those Sunday evenings, slide behind the long, red sofa, thence under the piano, to sit hidden behind the music rack and listen. Of course some of the guests spied me and were amused enough not to tell; it was not until I myself confessed that Mother learned I was not in bed asleep during these musical evenings.

One afternoon my closest friend, a "poor little rich girl," came to play; our great joy was to dress up in Mother's old evening clothes, and we both much preferred my parents' small apartment to her parents' enormous, Italianate mansion. That day for some reason her mother came to call for her, instead of the usual nurse or governess. My mother was playing the piano, and Mrs. W. stood for a long time outside the front door, listening. When she came in she told Mother that she was a friend of George Gershwin's, and that he was looking for someone to play two piano with, and suggested that Mother was just the person. "I was too shy," Mother told me later. "It's one of the greatest regrets of my life."

How do I reconcile my mother then and my mother now?

One evening before dinner Bion puts on Ravel's *Bolero.* We manage not to groan. How many times have we heard it? It's been a favorite of his ever since he discovered music. I look at Mother and wonder if there is a flicker of remembrance about the evening in Paris when she and Father heard *Bolero* performed for the first time ever, anywhere. We are so familiar with its repetitive, hypnotic rhythm that it is impossible for me to imagine hearing it completely freshly. Mother said that after the last long mesmerizing note died away the audience sat silent, stunned, and then burst into roars of cheering.

Another first performance at which she was present was that of César Franck's Symphony in D minor. This time the response was not applause but boos, and it was Hector Berlioz who led the audience in the heckling. A friend of Franck's went backstage and asked him how the symphony had sounded, and Franck smiled gently and said that it sounded just as he had hoped it would.

It is as difficult to imagine booing such melodious music as it is to imagine never having heard *Bolero.* But Mother was there, and her response was eternal dislike of Berlioz and a closed ear to all his music. His behavior and his composing were coupled forever in her mind. She wanted the artists she admired to be perfect in all ways, and it always upset her that her adored Wagner was "such a horrid man."

Last summer there were many evenings when the past was still available to her, and mornings when we sat together to drink our coffee and she could still tell me stories. She used to be a witty conversationalist, and I could get her out of bed by saying, "Mother, you have to help me. I've got things to do in the kitchen, and I can't leave the guests alone." Like an old race horse at the sound of the bell she would go into the living room, and from the kitchen I could hear laughter, and know that all was well. Not so this summer. She talks very little. It is all turned in, and it goes nowhere. She is trapped in a lonely, fearful present.

I want to open her memory, but I don't have the password. I want to cry out, "Open, sesame!" so that the door to this treasure cave will open, but it is permanently locked.

After dinner the girls get her ready for bed, and then I go to sit with her for a few minutes. The prevailing westerly wind has dropped, and it is unusually hot for our house on the hill. I sit there, not talking, holding Mother's hand, and remember another hot evening, in the apartment in New York, when I was a small child. Mother was sitting on the side of my bed, much as I now sit by her, stroking my head and pushing my perspiration-damp hair back from my forehead.

In the hall, between my parents' room and mine, hung an old etching of Castle Conway, in Wales. It's a charming picture, and I have always loved it because of the story my mother told me about it that night. It was probably the heat which reminded her, and my usual demand, "Tell me a story about you and Father." One hot summer evening, long before I was born, she walked through the hall and glanced at the etching of Castle Conway and said, "Oh, Charles, it's so hot. I wish we could go to Castle Conway." "Come on!" he cried, and swept her out of the house without toothbrush or change of clothes, and into a taxi, and by midnight they were on a ship sailing across the Atlantic. In those days a trip could be as spontaneous as that. My parents were not poor, but neither were they, by today's standards, affluent. Father was a playwright and journalist, and their pocketbook waned and swelled like the moon; this must have been one of the full-moon moments.

I hold my mother's hand and ask her, "Do you remember the time you and Father went to Castle Conway?"

She has forgotten, she who so short a time ago still remembered everything, and it troubles her, so I change the subject.

Her loss of memory is the loss of her self, her uniqueness, and this frightens me, for myself, as well as for her. Memory is probably my most essential tool as a storyteller, and the creative use of memory takes structure, enormous, disciplined structure, in a world where structure is unfashionable. Like the Red King, I'm apt to remember inaccurately what I don't write down in journal or notebook. "The horror of that moment," the king went on, "I shall never, *never* forget." "You will, though," the queen said, "if you don't make a memorandum of it."

Will I ever forget the intenseness of my anxiety about Hugh? Relief is already blunting the so-recent fear. I am already relaxing into the casual acceptance of a husband. Sooner or later I will get cross with him again, lose my temper, get hurt by something trivial. But I am sure that I shall never, *never* quite forget, and the setting down of the panic in my journal as well as my heart may be what will keep me from ever again taking a husband I love for granted.

And my mother's loss of memory will keep me from taking memory for granted.

Who is this cross old woman for whom I can do nothing right? I don't know her. She is not my mother. I am not her daughter. She won't eat anything I cook, so we resort to games. I do the cooking as usual—and I'm quite a good cook; it's one of my few domestic virtues, and the only part of housekeeping which I enjoy—and someone will say, "Eat Alan's soup, Grandmother. You know you like Alan's soup." Or, "Have some of Hugh's delicious salad." She won't eat the salad, when Hugh is in New York, until we tell her that Hugh made the dressing before he left.

I know that it is a classic symptom of atherosclerosis, this turning against the person you love most, and this knowledge is secure above my eyebrows, but very shaky below. There is something atavistic in us which resents, rejects, this reversal of roles. I want my mother to be my mother.

And she is not. Not any more. Not ever again.

8

I GO SEARCHING FOR HER.

My first memories of her are early, and are memories of smell, that oft-neglected sense, which is perhaps the first sense we use fully. Mother always smelled beautiful. I remember burrowing into her neck just for the soft loveliness of scented skin.

After smell came sound, the sound of her voice, singing to me, talking. I took the beauty of her voice for granted until I was almost grown up.

Scent. Sound. Vision.

I remember going into her room just before dinner, when she was sitting at her dressing table, rubbing sweet-smelling creams and lotions into her face. She had a set of ivory rollers from Paris, which I liked to play with; and a silver-backed nail buffer. Sometimes she let me buff my own nails until they were a pearly pink. The cake of French rouge, and the buffing, makes for a much prettier nail than lacquer.

I watched her brush her hair, a dark mahogany with red glints, thick and wavy, with a deep widow's peak. On the bed her evening dress was laid out; I remember one of flowered chiffon, short in front and long in back, that short-lived style of the twenties. Her shoes were bronze kid, and as tiny as Cinderella's.

My father, too, dressed for dinner every night, even when they were not having company or going out. Mother said that Father would dress for dinner in the desert or the jungle, and that he often told her that without him she'd be on the beach in two weeks. I doubt that. Until recently, I have never seen her anything but immaculate, erect, patrician. Now she has diminished; she is tiny and slumped and we have to dress her and fix her hair, but she is aware that she still has beautiful legs and she likes to show them. She responds to men, and she likes young people, which is not unusual.

Her father, my grandfather, who died at a hundred and one, responded to women and liked young people. One of the worst things about our attitude toward old people is the assumption that they ought to be herded together with other old people. Grandfather lived past that stage; he had, as he remarked, no contemporaries. He played golf until he was ninety-five, having cut down, at ninety, from thirty-six holes to eighteen because his younger companions couldn't keep up with him. He made the great mistake of retiring at ninety-five, and from then on began the slide into senility.

My mother tended him, with considerable assistance. Nevertheless, the psychological drain was on her, and it told in other ways, too. She has never been very strong, and several times during Grandfather's last years she told me that she did not think she would live to be very old. "But I don't want to," she added. "Don't grieve for me if I die. I don't ever want to be like Papa."

"Of course I'll grieve for you. But I don't want you to be like Grandfather, either."

Grandfather was dominant, powerful, ruthless, charming, wicked, brilliant, made and spent fortunes. It was strange to see the great man becoming an ancient baby. One night when he was around a hundred, Mother was sitting with him after he'd been put to bed, sitting with her father much as I now sit with my mother. He clasped her hand tightly, looked at her like a child, and asked, "Who is going to go with me when I die?"

We bring nothing with us into the world, and certainly we can take nothing out. We die alone. But I wish that most deaths today did not come in nursing homes or in hospitals. Death is an act which should not happen in such brutal settings. Future generations may well regard our hospitals and "rest" homes and institutions for the mentally ill with as much horror as we regard Bedlam.

Meanwhile, at Crosswicks I blunder along, and will continue to blunder as long as I can, although I am well aware that at the end of the summer there will be decisions to be made. Several years ago I promised Mother that I would never put her in a nursing home, and I may have to break that promise, deny what I affirm, because I will have no choice.

Her first night in Crosswicks this summer I called Vicki and Janet aside. "Sometimes at night Grandmother rings her bell too late, and can't make it to the bathroom in time. If this happens, call me. You're only supposed to listen for her at night, and take her to the bathroom if she needs to go, not to clean up if she's—incontinent."

Incontinent. I hesitated over the word. And my motives in telling the girls to call me if Mother soils herself were certainly mixed—but then, I have never had a completely unmixed motive in my life.

Part of it was consideration for the girls. They are not being paid to take over the more unpleasant parts of nursing. Another reason is that I did not want anybody to witness the humiliation of my aristocratic mother.

The girls do not call me. Almost every morning when I come hurrying downstairs they are washing the great-grandmother, changing the sheets—the washing machine goes constantly, sheets, diapers, work clothes—I am very grateful, this summer, for all my mechanical kitchen and laundry helpers. The girls are patient and gentle with Mother. I think they, too, feel that this is an unfair ploy on the part of life; it is wrong that we should lose control of our most private functions.

Old age has been compared to being once again like a baby; it is called second childhood. It is not. It is something very different. Charlotte is not yet two, and not yet completely toilet trained. Her soiled diapers have the still-innocuous odor of a baby's. As we grow older we, as well as our environment, become polluted. The smell of both urine and feces becomes yearly stronger.

In hospitals, in nursing homes, when people become incontinent this weakness is used against them. We have all heard far too many tales of elderly patients ringing for the bedpan, waiting fifteen minutes, half an hour, and finally not being able to control themselves any longer; and then, when the overworked nurse eventually arrives, the patient is scolded for lack of control.

There are not enough nurses, or aides, or orderlies. A hospital is no longer a good place for a person who is ill. I have my own account. After the birth of our first child, during the postwar boom of babies in the late 1940's, the eminent gynecologist who delivered Josephine did not check the placenta, and a large amount remained inside me. Three and a half weeks later, I hemorrhaged massively and was rushed to the hospital in the middle of the night. In this enlightened twentieth century I had childbed fever, and came very close to dying. One night I rang for the bedpan and, after waiting for over an hour, I wet the bed. And was roundly berated. I was young enough to fight back.

Mother is beyond that, and the idea of having her abused over a soiled bed is one of many reasons why putting her in a hospital or nursing home is still impossible to me.

One morning I dress Mother in a fresh nightgown while Vicki and Janet finish with the bed. Most mornings, Mother hardly seems to notice what has happened, or to care. She will murmur, "I'm cold. I want to go back to bed"—she who used to be so fastidious, so sweet-smelling. But this morning as I sit with my arms around her while the girls ready the bed, she leans against me and, suddenly herself, she says, "Oh, darling, I'm so ashamed about everything."

My heart weeps.

9

THEN THE CLOUDS close over again, and it is a bad day, a bad evening. She balks at going into the dining room and, once there, refuses to eat. She picks up her empty salad plate and there is a wild gleam in her eye as she says, "I can break this plate if I want to."

I say, "But you don't want to, Mother." It would be better to keep my mouth shut. But this is my mother, my rational, courteous, Southern gentlewoman mother, behaving in this irrational manner.

After dinner I call the dogs and go down the lane and weep. I have done a lot of crying on the lane. I cried whenever a book was rejected with an impersonal printed rejection slip. I cried when Hugh and I had a misunderstanding. Now I cry because I want my mother to die.

And I cry out of fear for myself. Will I ever be like that, a travesty of a person? It was the last thing she would have wanted, to live in this unliving, unloving manner. I look up at the sky and shout at the stars, "Take her, God! Take her!"

A few days ago I asked our doctor and friend, "John, is Mother dying?"

"Nature is not that kind. Your mother's blood pressure is better than yours."

Mine tends to drop when I'm tired; probably better than if it rose.

John suggested that we rent a hospital bed to make caring for her easier. How long is this going to go on? Is it fair to subject the entire family to this? What is it doing to the little girls? They have already experienced a different kind of death, in moving here from England, from Lincoln, the only home they have known. Léna said goodbye to her English great-grandmother. "We're going to America, and we'll never, ever see you again." True, but it didn't go down very well.

In the spring Josephine had a miscarriage, and this death, for the children, was not so much the death of a tiny, unformed life they had never known, as the fact that their mother, the foundation of their world, could be suddenly and without warning taken from them. Will it wound them or strengthen them to be in this house this summer?

It's one thing for me. I'm the only child. Is it fair to make the whole family suffer for what I believe? I talked awhile, earlier this summer, about wanting my mother to have a dignified death. But there is nothing dignified about incontinence and senility.

She is *my* mother. I have no brothers and sisters with whom to share responsibilities and decisions. The others, no matter how close, are at one remove at least. Have I the right to drag them through this with me? It is, in any case, not only my decision. The entire household is involved. After our discussions we come to no decisions, but I feel sustained and supported. We have talked today, in the hot sunlight, on this lane where I am walking now in the starlight. The strength of the family gives me strength. The dogs know that I am upset, and I do not mind letting go in front of them. They dash down the lane, into the bushes, circle back, and sniff me anxiously. Their concern makes me break into a loud sob, and Tyrrell leaps to give my wet face a loving lick. We are too far from the house for anybody to hear me, but it is time for me to dry my eyes and go home.

I learned several years ago that a four-generation summer can be a good one only if we all have our own survival routines. Each one of us must manage to find a time of solitude and privacy. Hugh, when he is in Crosswicks, goes to his garden. Alan goes out to the Tower to read and write. I do not want to take my pain out on the rest of the family, so every afternoon, before time to cook dinner, I go across the fields to the brook, pushing through the tall grass nearly ready for its first haying, with the dogs circling joyfully about me. When I am out of sight Mother is apt to send for me. "Where's Madeleine? Get Madeleine." At the brook I'm beyond the reach of even a loud shout. If anybody really wants me, somebody has to come fetch me.

I used to feel guilty about spending morning hours working on a book; about fleeing to the brook in the afternoon. It took several summers of being totally frazzled by September to make me realize that this was a false guilt. I'm much more use to family and friends when I'm not physically and spiritually depleted than when I spend my energies as though they were unlimited. They are not. The time at the typewriter and the time at the brook refresh me and put me into a more workable perspective.

Across the brook is a stone bridge; it is not a natural bridge; it was put there a century or more ago by skillful hands and no modern stone-moving tools. It was probably part of one of the early roads, barely wide enough for a single horse and rider. I sit on it and dangle my legs over the gentle flowing of the water, shaded by maple and beech, birch and ash trees. I need perspective, and how to find it? caught in the middle of things, never quite able to avoid subjectivity, or to get the thinking me and the feeling me to coincide.

This makes me confused, makes me lose sight of reality. I feel my lacks as wife, daughter, mother; and if I dwell too much on my lacks they become even greater, and I am further from—not just reality, but the truth of this summer. Will I ever know it?

When Josephine was just a year old, I spent most of the summer alone at Crosswicks because Hugh was off working at various summer theatres, and Mother had broken her ankle in the spring and so could not join us until August. During these solitary weeks I wrote a full first draft of a book. It was my fourth full-length novel, and I had reluctantly put the third on the shelf, after many revisions; so I felt especially precarious about the summer's work, and I knew that how I would feel about that particular summer for the rest of my life was going to depend on what happened with my manuscript.

The book was well received by the publisher and—eventually—the press, and is still, after all these years, selling. And so, I remember that summer as a "good" summer. If the book had been rejected, it would be forever in my memory a "bad" summer. That's irrational, but it's the way things are.

So what of the verisimilitude of that long-gone summer? Do I know it at all? It was a time of solitude, rather than loneliness, because I was happy with my writing, happy with my baby. But what was it *really* like? I don't know.

So I will probably never fathom the reality of this summer. What is the truth of the ninety-year-old woman waiting for me at the house, who is changed beyond recognition and yet who is still my mother?

For a human being, truth is verisimilitude, a likeness to what is real, which is as close as we can get to reality. It has taken me many years to learn that reality is far more than meets the human eye, or ear, or mind, and that the greatest minds have never attained more than fragmentary flashes of what is really real.

Below me on a flat, mossy stone in the brook sits a small green frog. What is a frog? What is the reality of a frog? I was fascinated by a scientific article which showed pictures of a frog as seen by a human eye, by a bird's eye, by a snake's eye. Each saw a very different creature. Which frog was more real?

All of us in Crosswicks this summer see a different person when we look at my mother. Vicki and Janet and Margie have known her all their lives, as Jo's and Maria's and Bion's grandmother. For my children, she has been a very special grandmother. When Josephine had mononucleosis the first winter of her marriage, she didn't get well until she was sent down to Grandmother to be petted and pampered and cosseted. Bion, each spring vacation, says,

"I have to go South for a week with Grandmother." I know a very different person from the one my children do. I know only a fragment of this old lady. She is far more than I can begin to understand. She was fifty-five when my father died; the woman he was married to for nearly thirty years is not the woman I know. I have pictures of her when she was a baby, a young girl, a bride, but this past of my mother's is beyond my comprehension. I am far from understanding her reality.

The Greeks come to my help again; they have a word for the realness of things, the essence of a frog, of the stone bridge I am sitting on, of my mother: *ousia.*

If I am to be constant in loving and honoring my mother I must not lose sight of *ousia.* It's a good word; it's my new word. Last summer my word was *ontology:* the word about being. This summer I need to go a step further, to *ousia,* the essence of being, to that which is really real.

The frog makes a small, clunking noise and hops to another stone and sits, his pale green throat pulsing. He *is:* frog: unworried by the self-consciousness with which the human animal is stuck; it is our blessing and our curse; not only do we know, we know that we know. And we are not often willing to face how little we know.

I learn slowly, and always the hard way. Trying to be what I am not, and cannot be, is not only arrogant, it is stupid. If I spend the entire day hovering around Mother, trying to be the perfect daughter, available every time she asks, "Where's Madeleine?"; if I get up early with my grandbabies and then stay up late with my actor husband and get no rest during the day; if I have no time in which to write; if I make myself a martyr to appease my false guilt, then I am falling into the age-old trap of pride. I fall into it too often.

A conversation with a friend helped open my eyes. Connie is about ten years older than I am, and her mother died a year ago, and Connie is filled with guilt. Now I happen to know that Connie was more than just a dutiful daughter; she kept her mother at home until a hospital was inevitable; she visited her daily thereafter; the difficult old woman was treated with love and kindness; and I told Connie that if anybody had little cause for guilt, it was she. But the guilt was obviously there, and a sore weight. So I said that we all, all of us without exception, have cause for guilt about our parents, and that I had far more cause than she. Then I heard myself saying, "I don't think real guilt is ever much of a problem for us. It's false guilt that causes the trouble." Connie gave me a funny, surprised look, and said, "I think you're right."

And a load of guilt fell from my own shoulders.

I certainly have legitimate cause for both real and false guilt with my mother. But when I try to be the perfect daughter, to be in control of the situation, I become impaled on false guilt and become overtired and irritable.

It is only by accepting real guilt that I am able to feel free of guilt as I sit on the stone bridge and cool my feet in the dappled shade and admire the pop eyes of the frog; and it comes to me that if I am not free to accept guilt when I do wrong, then I am not free at all. If all my mistakes are excused, if there's an alibi, a rationalization for every blunder, then I am not free at all. I have become subhuman.

At best I am far from a perfect wife, or mother,

or daughter. I do all kinds of things which aren't right, which aren't sensitive or understanding. I neglect all kinds of things which I ought to do. But Connie made me realize that one reason I don't feel guilty is that I no longer feel I have to be perfect. I am not in charge of the universe, whereas a humanist has to be, and when something goes wrong, tiny, delicate Connie, like most convinced humanists I've known, becomes enclosed with self-blame because she can't cope with the situation, and this inability presents her with a picture of herself which is not the all-competent, in-control-of-everything person she wants to see.

It is a trap we all fall into on occasion, but it is particularly open to the intelligent atheist. There is no God, and if there is, he's not arranging things very well; therefore, I must be in charge. If I don't succeed, if I am not perfect, I carry the weight of the whole universe on my shoulders.

And so the false guilt which follows the refusal to admit any failure is inevitable.

10

IT IS ONLY WHEN I can shake off the load of false guilt that I can contemplate death. I do not like thinking about death. I am bad about death. Death is not—despite the Romantics—natural. Death is the enemy, and I hate it. My only weapon against death is to do my dying freely, consciously. This summer is practice in dying for me as well as for my mother.

Our lives are a series of births and deaths: we die to one period and must be born to another. We die to childhood and are born to adolescence; to our high-school selves and (if we are fortunate) to our college selves; we die to our college selves and are born into the "real" world; to our unmarried selves and into our married. To become a parent is birth to a new self for the mother and father as well as for the baby. When Hugh and I moved from the city to live year round at Crosswicks, this was death to one way of life and birth to another. Then nine years later when we took our children, aged seven, ten, and twelve, out of a big house, a quiet village, a small country school, and moved back to New York and the world of the theatre, this was another experience of death and birth.

Both life and death are present for me in the house this summer. I look at Mother, and think that if I am to reflect on the eventual death of her body, of all bodies, in a way that is not destructive, I must never lose sight of those other deaths which precede the final, physical death, the deaths over which we have some freedom; the death of self-will, self-indulgence, self-deception, all those self-devices which, instead of making us more fully alive, make us less.

The times I have been most fully me are when I have been wholly involved in someone or something else; when I am listening, rather than talking; cooking a special, festive dinner; struggling with a fugue at the piano; putting a baby to bed; writing. A long-dead philosopher said that if we practice dying enough during our lives we will hardly notice the moment of transition when the actual time comes. But I am far from a saint, and I am seldom able to practice consciously this kind of dying; it is not a do-it-yourself activity. I know about it only after it has happened, and I am only now beginning to recognize it for what it is.

It has nothing to do with long-faced self-righteousness, with pomposity or piousity. It does not preclude play or laughter. It is light, not heavy; merry, not sad; and it is realistic and never sentimental.

Our lives are given a certain dignity by their very evanescence. If there were never to be an end to my quiet moments at the brook, if I could sit on the rock forever, I would not treasure these minutes so much. If our associations with the people we love were to have no termination, we would not value them as much as we do. Human love is an extraordinary gift, but like all flesh it is corruptible. Death or distance separates all lovers. My awareness of my husband is sharpened by impermanence.

Would we really value anything we could have forever and ever? This is not the first time death has come close to my heart. I was close to the deaths of my grandparents, my father, many relatives and friends. When Hugh and I were in our early thirties, four of our closest friends died, people who were so intimate a part of our lives that their dying changed the very fabric of our days. All four of these deaths were unexpected, and only Don, a fine actor in his seventies, was not cut off *in medias res*.

Of these four deaths the one which changed our lives most irrevocably was Liz's, because it brought seven-year-old Maria into our family.

Our phone rang one quiet January evening while we were getting ready for dinner. If *The Magic Flute* will always mean Crosswicks and Margie; if the Tallis *Variations* will always mean this one particular summer; Glück's *Orpheo ed Euridice* will always remind me of Arthur, because it was on the record player when the phone rang. I answered, and Liz said, "Arthur's dead."

The next day she came up with Maria, leaving her with us for a month while she tried to get things in order. Arthur had left no will; his business, a small publishing house, had been largely in his head. Liz and Arthur had a joint bank account and at Arthur's death it was frozen; Liz had only the money in her pocket, and had to borrow from friends to get through the next few weeks.

During the summer Maria came to us again. All of Maria's few birthdays had been in Crosswicks, so we had the usual party under the apple trees, with balloons and presents tied to the branches, turning the tiny orchard into birthday trees. Before her wedding, Maria told me that the birthday trees are one of the happiest memories of her childhood, and this warms the cockles of my heart.

Liz came up to Crosswicks to get Maria, and to rest for a few days. One evening toward bedtime, we went outdoors to watch for shooting stars and to talk. There was a bite in the air, and we took blankets and wore elderly fur coats which would be rejected by any thrift shop, coats we keep in the pantry hall for dog walking and star watching.

We lay on the lawn on the north of the house, looking across a large pasture to the trees and the hills beyond. Liz told me that Arthur's estate was almost settled, thanks to a lawyer friend, and that he had also drawn up a will for her. She was preparing to start rehearsals in an excellent role in a play that had every smell of a hit, and she was beginning to look toward the future with eagerness. She had left the theatre when Maria was born; she was returning now both because acting was her joy and because it was the way she had been trained to earn her living.

A bright star fizzed across the sky and went out.

Then Liz said, "If anything should happen to me—not that I expect it to—but if anything should, would you and Hugh take care of Maria? I know you love her, and would bring her up the way I want."

I told Hugh about the conversation and we forgot about it until the following November, one morning before dawn when the phone rang. The phone is on Hugh's side of the bed, and he answered it.

A phone call at that time of day usually means something wrong, and I could tell from Hugh's shocked voice that it was not a wrong number or anything unimportant. He said, "Liz is dead."

During rehearsal the day before, she had been

stricken by a bad headache which rapidly became worse. It was finally so bad that the stage manager took her home in a cab. Her mother was minding Maria, and opened the door. The stage manager said, reassuringly, "It's a bad headache. The theatre doctor has given her some medication, and she'll feel better soon."

It was not just a bad headache; it was a cerebral hemorrhage, and Liz was dead before morning.

Liz died on the twenty-sixth of November. The funeral was on the twenty-ninth: my birthday.

We drove down to New York to the funeral home. Funeral "home"—another obscenity. Right after the service, Maria came up to me and caught hold of my hand and would not let go. When it came time to leave the cloying and fetid atmosphere of the funeral home, Maria kept repeating to anyone who came near her, "I'm staying with Aunt Madeleine. I'm going where she goes. I'm not going anywhere she doesn't go. I'm staying with her."

So Hugh and I, Maria, and Ezra, the lawyer who had been so helpful to Liz, went to a nearby restaurant for something to eat, and Ezra disappeared. We didn't know where he'd gone, or why, and just as we were beginning to wonder, he walked in, saying, "We couldn't just let your birthday go by," and handed me a corsage, and a rosebud for Maria.

Late that night, back in Goshen, I wrote, "Let me start now to write a little about the events of the past hours—and one of the strangest birthdays I ever had." I wrote about the funeral, and the lunch, and then going back to the apartment with Maria. I'd climbed up the several flights of stairs with Maria still holding tightly to my hand, and I recorded in my journal some of the things she said. "Can I come live with you? . . . Can I live with you forever and ever? . . . Can I spend next Christmas with you? and the next? and the next? and the next? I hope . . . I'd like to adopt you. Do you think you could adopt me? . . . Would Mommy want me to come live with you? . . . Will Bion and Jo be my real brother and sister, then?" She was grasping for answers, for reassurance. Her grandmother had asked her, "Do you want to come to your mother's funeral, Maria? Of course you don't have to come if you don't want to, but you can come if you like." What a responsibility to put on an already shocked seven-year-old!

I wrote the next day, "I know I've left out all kinds of important things, but it's terribly difficult to write with so many interruptions, and besides we're terribly tired still, emotionally and mentally.

"We got home around five o'clock and Hugh went right to the store and I got dinner. It was choir night, so I knew we'd have to hurry. While I was getting dinner the phone rang; one of our close friends had been rushed to Boston for emergency surgery for an intestinal stoppage. My heart began to thud: O God, not something else! Even after her husband had assured me that the operation had been successful and she was going to be all right, I still felt panic at the ruthlessness of fate, and our total inability to stop the phone ringing with a message of another tragedy. Meanwhile, I must seem as normal as possible for the children, who are very shaken by the death of the beautiful woman they called Aunt Liz."

I wrote, "We had a steak for dinner to mark my birthday, and then I dashed over to choir, and it was a good rehearsal, and as I dismissed them, Grandma [who has played the church organ for seventy plus years and is called Grandma by us all] started to play 'Happy Birthday,' and everybody sang, and Gill said I got bright pink. I said I couldn't think of a nicer way to spend my birthday than directing choir, and then Herb said, 'Look who's here,' and there was Hugh standing in the doorway and I said, 'What are you doing here!' and it was for birthday cake and tea and coffee downstairs. What a darling thing for them to do! The birthday cake had *'Happy birthday, Boss'* on it, and Ella had set the table prettily, and the whole thing gave me a warm glow and somehow made the whole day seem all right.

"Today has been cold and raw. I wrote another number for the operetta—how do people who don't have work bear things? . . . The moment I felt the loss of Liz most was Wednesday evening, walking from the parking lot on Thirteenth Street to Sixteenth Street . . . I'd left the car there so often and then walked over to Liz's, and suddenly I realized what had happened and that it was never to be again, and felt my first real rush of grief . . . I'm bone-tired but I must write to Maria. Tired and let-down and tense and sad and depressed. . . ."

There were a number of unexpected problems to be overcome before Maria could come to us, and she had an extremely upsetting several weeks, including Christmas, until I was abruptly telephoned, on the morning of January 5, to come down to New York—one hundred miles—and fetch her.

When we got back to Crosswicks late that afternoon, there was a small shape huddled in the back of our garage; it was Bella, a seventeen-year-old girl who used to babysit for us until her family moved away when she was fifteen. She sat waiting for us on an old tricycle, shivering in an inadequate coat, pregnant, and unmarried. So our family increased rapidly. It is odd how large events are indicated by small ones. The first difference I noticed was how quickly the toilet paper and toothpaste got used up.

Worrying about Maria and Bella usurped all other emotion, so that I had no time to grieve for Liz, a grieving that is still to be done. We can put off such essential acts when necessary, but not indefinitely. During the years of our friendship Liz and I talked as only friends of the right hand can talk; she took a goodly number of confidences of mine to the grave with her; I carry secrets of hers locked in my heart. When I pass her picture each day I feel a brief, almost unacknowledged stab.

I lie back on the rock which holds the warmth of the sun and look up at the sky. The clouds are moving across the heat-hazy blue from the northwest: good weather tomorrow. A hawk breaks across the sky with a powerful swoop. He is very sure of himself. I am not a hawk, and I will never be that certain.

But I am peaceful, lying on the rock for half an hour until time to return to the house and start dinner.

11

THE LIFE OF AN ACTOR is sometimes considered to be unreal, to be a sham. But I have been close to many actors and actresses and they have made me feel that an actor in his various roles is trying on aspects of himself, is trying to find out who he is, what is the nature of humankind, much as I struggle with the same questions through the characters in my stories. If the actor plunges into this openly and vulnerably, he shares his discoveries with the audience; his insights become ours. I have learned both about Hugh and about myself from his "play acting." From a presidential candidate to a fifteenth-century cardinal to a twentieth-century con man, he moves with ease and grace, and I discover things about him in this way that I might never learn in the ordinary process of daily living. This summer we turn television on every day to watch Hugh as an urbane, ever courteous physician, Dr. Charles Tyler. The television set is in Mother's room and she would not miss this program. But one day she refuses to acknowledge that the man on the screen is Hugh. "That is not Hugh," she announces in her most authoritarian way. "That is somebody else pretending to be Hugh." Nobody can convince her. I'm glad that I am not alone in saying, "But it *is* Hugh." She is so definite that I almost find myself wondering.

How do I know that Hugh is Hugh and not anybody else? That I am me? That this stranger questioning my husband's identity is my mother? Suddenly the whole structure of human identity seems precarious, but perhaps part of my confusion is caused by fatigue. Last night was another of those nights when I couldn't help staying awake almost all night, listening. Mother was calling out, and I had to decide each time whether or not to go downstairs. Mostly I thought she was calling in her sleep, and not really wanting anyone. She can still find her buzzer, or call the girls. What I listen for is fear in her voice, because I cannot bear the thought of having her afraid alone in the night.

But for me to stay awake all night, fearful of her fear, is folly. Janet and Vicki are on folding cots in the living room, by the open door. There is only the narrow, New England front hall between living room and Mother's open bedroom door. The two girls are there to tend Grandmother, as they call her. They are there so that the rest of us can sleep. For me to spend half the night up on my elbow, listening, is sheer stupidity. I'll never last the summer this way, and what good will that do Mother?

In the Tower there is a couch which pulls out from under the eaves to become a double bed. The only sensible thing for me to do from now on is to sleep out there, the one place where I can't hear everything that is going on in the house; sensible not only for my sake but for Mother's, for the whole household.

But her fears concern me, and I don't know how to assuage them. Far too often during the day, especially as she is being moved from her bed to the big chair by the window in the kitchen, she will repeat, like a needle stuck in one groove on a record, "I'm afraid, I'm afraid, I'm afraid." She cannot tell us what she's afraid of, except falling. We all promise her that we won't let her fall. "It's all right, Grandmother. We're with you, we'll hold you. It's all right."

It is an instinctive refrain, even in the very young girls. We are surely promising her more than that we won't let her fall; perhaps the girls aren't aware of all that they imply, but it is in their voices. It is in mine, and I have certainly learned that "Mother," no matter how much she may want to, cannot stop accidents, cannot stop war, cannot stop death, cannot control the future. I am promising something beyond all this; I am promising a reasonable and loving power behind the creation of the universe, and this is something I am going to have to think about, and to question.

Whenever possible, two of us move the great-grandmother, one on each side, holding her close and tight. I hope that the constant physical support will give her some of the spiritual support she needs, because her fears are as much of the future as they are of falling. When her mind clears at all, she is afraid of the trip back South, and I am convinced that she cannot make it; it took too much out of her to come to Crosswicks, and she has failed radically since then. All we can do is try to ease her fear, her fear of leaving us, not to take the plane down South, but leaving us to go into the unknown country of death. She used to tell me that she was not afraid of death, but "I'm afraid of the mechanics of dying." Yet *timor mortis* is in her now, unspoken, but apparent to us all.

During the day the big chair is the best place for

her, because she is part of all the household there. The windows in the dining half of the kitchen are an expanse of about fifteen feet, and from them she can watch Hugh working in the garden, watch the babies on their swings or in their little paddle pool. She can look through the open doorway into the living room, where Margie is polishing brass. She can see me at the stove, or cleaning vegetables in the long sink. Josephine or Alan will read to her, or try to talk to her. Clara brushes her hair, still thick and white and wavy and beautiful, until she relaxes under the gentleness and forgets her fear. When Maria and Peter are with us they, too, try to keep her in life. A great deal of the time she watches nothing, but nods in her chair, and doesn't even notice the usual kitchen noisiness, babies, pots and pans, the pantry door which doesn't shut unless it's slammed loudly, conversations, snatches of song . . .

This morning I said to Clara that Mother has often wished she could die like Grandfather, just turn over in bed and die, and we both agreed that if she could do just that, it would be the best possible thing. She is older at ninety than Grandfather was at a hundred. After the big one-hundredth birthday party, Grandfather decided to die, and it took him just a little over a year to wind down. Mother is fighting, fighting death, fighting us. Last night she started to throw a fork at Bion; fortunately her hand picked up her napkin instead. She makes wild accusations. "How can anybody be so cruel to anybody? My own daughter, how can anybody be so cruel?"

I am foolish enough to be hurt, even though I know that the *ousia* of my mother could never say such a thing, that she has always loved me and always will. Part of what she is doing now is an act, put on for Josephine and Alan's benefit or anybody else available to be an audience, but only part; in any case, it's an act she's not responsible for, and can't control. She is no longer able to govern what is happening in her brain. There are only the rarest, briefest flashes of a person in this huddled, frightened, frightening, ancient woman.

I begin to understand that her atypical rage is an instinctive rebellion against her total inability to control what is going on in the arteries of her brain. We have learned that when any group of people is oppressed for too long, no matter how peaceable they may be natively, powerlessness and impotence will eventually lead to violence. Surely Mother's outbursts of violence come from that part of her subconscious mind which still functions through the devouring of arteries by atherosclerosis. It is frustration which sparks the wild rage.

And my own angers startle me. My boiling point seems to get lower day by day, and it is small, unimportant things which cause the volcano to erupt.

This summer, when writing is next to impossible, walking the dogs to the brook is my outlet. Sometimes I cry out at the imperturbable green surrounding me: "How can you let something like this happen to my mother? Why can't you let her die!"

A bird gives a call and flies off. The throat of the little green frog flutters with anxiety, and I quiet down. But if I get it out of me this way, I'm not as apt to take it out on the family. Out it has to get, one way or another. I do not understand why it is not, as usual, work on a book. Most of the time I can write my way through anything; I have written some of my best poems in hospitals, waiting for X rays; in the middle of the night when pain keeps me awake.

But my creative energy is being drained. When I was pregnant with Josephine, a friend who was a successful dancer and the mother of several children told me that a woman cannot be creative in two ways simultaneously, and that I would not be able to write while I was carrying the baby. Obviously she could not do a *tour jeté* when she was five months pregnant, but I saw no reason not to go on writing, and write I did. The odd thing is that nothing I wrote during my pregnancies ever came, itself, to term. It was like practicing finger exercises, absolutely essential for the playing of the fugue, but it did not lead to the fugue till after the baby was born. I do not understand this, but I do not think it coincidence.

In a reverse way, sharing my mother's long, slow dying consumes my creative energy. I manage one angry and bitter story, and feel better for it, but most of me is involved in Mother's battle. Watching her slowly being snuffed out is the opposite of pregnancy, depleting instead of fulfilling; I am exhausted by conflict.

Periodically I check with Dr. John. This morning he came and gave Mother a complete going over. We have known John and his family ever since we have been coming to Crosswicks; it was John who delivered Bion. He affirmed that Mother is, indeed, doing a good bit of play acting. She can't help it; she's playing games with all of us. He assured us that we are doing all we can, that we must continue to keep her moving, and to take her for a short walk in the afternoon to keep at least a little circulation going. I trust John, and I know that Mother can go on this way indefinitely. Nevertheless, I still see her as in the act of dying.

Alan says that one of the hardest things for all of us is the fear that one day we will be like this. Because I am already a grandmother, this fear is acute in me. It will be a long time before I am able to forget my mother as she is this summer, and remember her as she used to be.

I struggle for *ousia,* for that which does not change with the change and decay in all around I see. Small joys give me glimpses of reality, and keep me going. "Cammy me, Madden," says Charlotte, holding up her little arms. "You not going *anywhere,* Ganmadlen," says Léna, reaching out for security in an insecure world.

I learn from them; I learn from their great-grandmother's *terror anticus;* perhaps the forcible awareness of insecurity is one reason why I respond so deeply to the fugue. I should think that by now Hugh—and the rest of the family—would be sick and tired of Bach's C minor Toccata and Fugue, but it has pulled me through many bad moments, and helped express the joy of happy ones. If I leave Mother after a non-conversation which has me churning and out of proportion, the minutes of working through that particular fugue, which I am in the midst of memorizing, will bring me back into enough perspective so that I can return to Mother with love, instead of indulging in my own reactions. If I want an answer to my questions about all-rightness, all I need to do is play the C minor Fugue. The family knows how much the piano puts me into perspective. When I am overtly upset or angry, Bion will say, as to a child, "Why don't you go play the piano, Mother?"

It has been a long time since the great-grandmother played the piano, and I learned, in early adolescence, that when she played Bach for several hours, or when she played game after game of solitaire, she was unhappy; I was old enough to understand the fact of the unhappiness but not the reasons, and so got caught up in unhappiness too. Anyhow, I mustn't play the C minor too often this summer, and preferably only when the girls take Mother for her afternoon walk and she can't hear the powerful, austere interweaving of theme, and be reminded of unhappiness.

It is frightening to be in such a position of power over another human being that I must question even what I play on the piano. We are all in positions of power over the great-grandmother, and I know that I can trust this Crosswicks household not to abuse it. Vicki and Janet are unfailingly patient over soiled sheets. Clara will never pinch or hurt while the bath is being given, or be rough when she is brushing Mother's hair and keeping it fresh and clean. Daily I learn lessons in patience and forbearance. Margie questions me about forcing Grandmother to take the walk in the afternoon when she doesn't want to go. I explain that Dr. John has told us it is the only way to keep any blood circulating in the clogging arteries; it hurts me, too, to make my mother walk against her wishes. It would be easier to give in, and let her turn completely into a vegetable. "And that wouldn't be loving my mother, Margie." Slowly Margie nods. "Okay, Madeleine. I understand now."

I do not want power over my mother. I am her child; I *want* to be her child. Instead, I have to be the mother.

12

MEALS BECOME A NIGHTMARE. Finally, after discussion and support from the family, I decide that we will no longer try to make Mother eat. If her body really wants food, its want will be heard and she will take a few bites of baked potato. But we will stop this farce of urging her to eat, and I will not allow anybody to feed her as though she were a baby.

Do I have a right to make this decision? Perhaps not, but I make it because it is the decision I would want my children to make if I were in my mother's place. There is no dignity to this kind of death at best; but forcing food down her when she is not hungry is simply an added indignity.

The babies and the animals affirm the great-grandmother's reality in a way that I cannot, because they are able to take her for granted exactly as she is. This morning I watched Léna sitting in her small rocking chair at her great-grandmother's feet, sitting with a book of nursery rhymes held upside down, rocking and singing to her great-grandmother. Titus, the yellow kitten, curled up in the old woman's lap, yawned with luxurious contentment. For a brief moment I too could accept, and my heart was warm and freed from the numbness which has enclosed it most of the time during these weeks.

I read somewhere that the subconscious mind cannot understand or accept its own extinction. But I don't think that the conscious mind gets very close to understanding or acceptance either. It is a fact that all men must die; but because my underwater, subconscious mind, the largest part of me, does not believe it, my intellectual acceptance doesn't mean very much.

First of all, I don't know what death means:

Death first intruded upon me when I was three years old, and my paternal grandmother came to visit us in New York and died of pneumonia, in my bed, in my room. My memory of this death is two small fragments; I remember sitting on the floor beside the bed, playing with a pack of cards; it must have been before anybody realized that she was gravely ill. And I remember driving at night to her home, near Princeton, New Jersey; we passed road construction, and I remember the red lanterns hanging from the barriers blocking our way and the unknown dark ahead. After this, memory betrays me chronologically. Although I know we were driving to New Jersey for the funeral, my tricky memory projects me into the comfortable living room of my grandmother's house, and I am sitting in her ample lap, being rocked by her, and we are flooded with golden light from a Tiffany lampshade.

I was in early adolescence when my other grandmother, my maternal grandmother, died at the beach cottage in North Florida.

We had to drive from the beach up to town, and

I remember my sense of shock as we drove through the hot and crowded streets; the familiar city was new to me; it was as though I had never passed through these streets before. The entire world was different, and nobody we passed knew it; nobody knew that my grandmother had died; and this seemed to me outrageous.

It was more than a selfish, childish, reaction. Perhaps we are supposed to walk more often through the streets of that different world, where all our awareness is more acute, not our awareness of ourselves but an awareness that we *are* part of each other, that we are all as intricately and irrevocably connected as the strands of a fugue.

This is the world I walk in this summer.

This world is crystal-clear, and yet it is not bathed in the white light of intellectual certainty. It has more to do with the underwater world, the world in which I meet the characters and people of my stories, the world in which I understand the language of the C minor Fugue.

I first came across this fugue while I was in college during a time of confusion and unhappiness. I still had not come to terms with my father's death, which occurred during my last year in boarding school. It was a premature death, caused by mustard gas during the First World War; Father would not take his men anywhere he would not go himself, and his action saved most of his men from gassing. If my memory of Mother begins with smell and sound, so does my memory of Father: smell of clean linen, after-shave lotion, whiskey; sound of coughing.

And I was afraid of death, all death, afraid for

my mother, for myself. The C minor Fugue spoke to me in a language even more positive than that of John Donne's beautiful sonnet, "Death be not proud."

What do I believe, this summer, about death and the human being? I'm not sure. But I know that it is in the language of the fugue, not the language of intellectual certainty. And I know that I could not survive this summer if I could not hope for meaning, meaning to my mother's life, to Hugh's and mine, to our children's, to all the larger family, to everybody, to all things, including the rock at the brook and the small frog. What that ultimate meaning may be I do not know, because I am finite, and the meaning I hope for is not. But God, if he is God, if he is worth believing in, is a loving God who will not abandon or forget the smallest atom of his creation. And that includes my mother. And everybody, everybody without exception.

I cannot believe in meaning by myself, alone, but it is often the small things which sustain me. Someone will say, after a particularly difficult, tiring day, "Madeleine, dinner tonight was just great." Or I will sit, in the twilight, in the old rocker with one of the babies and sing, and take strength from the small and perfect body drooping into sleep in my arms. At least once a week Alan, or Tallis, will celebrate Communion, and from this I receive the same kind of strength which, in a different way, comes to me in the C minor Fugue, and I am able to return to the routine of these difficult days with a lighter touch.

Would I be able to go on, one day at a time, this way, if we lived in a small pre-fab house in Levittown, or a cramped apartment in the City? It would take a great deal more strength and courage than is being called from me here in Crosswicks, and there are days even here, even with the help of the household and the quiet minutes at the brook, when I am so exhausted by nighttime that I barely have the strength to climb the stairs to the Tower and fall into bed.

Somehow, despite the fact that I feel that my mother's slow dying and birth are opposites, I still turn to the analogy of birth. When I walk down the lane at night and pray for Mother's death, I must know what I am praying for, and I am praying not just for her release from the prison her body has been turned into, but for birth. Alan was with Josephine during Charlotte's birth, and was amazed not only by the violence with which the mother works to expel the baby but by the violence with which the baby struggles to be born. Charlotte—typically—did not need to be spanked into life; she emerged shouting. Only a few hours earlier she had been safely inside her mother's womb, swimming comfortably in the amniotic fluid. Everything was done for her; she was sustained and nourished in the dark warmth. And suddenly the calm waters started churning, and she was shoved through a dark tunnel into blinding light, air knifed into her unused lungs, and she greeted the trauma of birth with a bellow of rage.

It's a good analogy for me, birth, and certainly has nothing to do with pie in the sky by and by. Perhaps the great-grandmother is as much afraid of the violence of a new birth as she is of the act of dying.

Do I believe all this? Not with my intellect. But my intuition keeps insisting that there are more things on heaven and earth, Horatio, than your philosophies can tell.

I'll leave it there for now. The only thing to do is to get up in the morning and move through the day, trying to do what has to be done, as it comes. When Mother's face crumples pitifully and she says, "I'm scared, I'm scared," I put my arms around her and say, "It's all right, Mother," and I do this well aware of the enormity of the promise. There is a chill and empty feeling within me; nevertheless, there is something which impels me to put my arms around the Madeleine who is ninety and the Madeleine who has just turned three, and say, "Don't be afraid. It's all right."

II

The Mother I Knew

1

I WAS a much longed-for baby. It wasn't for want of trying that my parents were childless for so long. But Mother could not hold a baby past three months. "All I needed to get pregnant," she once remarked, "was for your father to hang his pajamas over the bedpost." She had miscarriages all over the world—Paris, Berlin, Cairo, and—I think—one in China. Sometime toward the end of "the war," my parents' war, World War I, Father came home on leave from Plattsburg, and I was conceived. Because Father was sent immediately overseas, Mother was able to spend most of the nine months in bed. Even so, I am a witness to her determination. The first doctor she went to told her that she could not possibly carry a baby to term, and that if she did not have a therapeutic abortion, both she and the baby would die. Then she went to a Roman Catholic doctor: that was in 1918. So I am here to tell the story.

My Southern grandmother, Dearma, came north to take care of her daughter. Mother carried me the full nine months, and started labor late on a blizzardy Thanksgiving night. Dearma went out onto Park Avenue to try to call a taxi to take Mother to the hospital, but the storm was so fierce that no taxis came by. There the elderly lady stood in the snow, wind blowing her clothes about her, whipping her white hair free of its pins, and finally two young men in a long touring car stopped and asked if she needed help. So my mother was driven to the hospital by two friendly strangers.

Father didn't see me until I was several months old, because he was kept overseas after the Armistice. I wish that we had not wiped out Armistice Day in favor of Veterans Day. It strikes me as part of our reluctance to accept the horrid reality of death. We are afraid of that dark silence when for a minute everybody in the nation was supposed to pause and think of the dead. And I remember the ancient verses,

The gude Sir Hew of Eglintoun,
And eik Heriot, and Wintoun,
He has tane out of this cuntre;
Timor mortis conturbat me.

And I add,

Remember Charles of Crosswicks town
And those beside him who went down.
The flesche is brukle, the Fiend is sle;
Timor mortis conturbat me.

I share in the primordial terror.

Otherwise I could not sit by my mother at night and hold her dry and burning hand in my still quick one. Her hand is as dry and fragile as a leaf in November.

She told me that once she and Father had had their long-awaited baby, I became a bone of contention between them. They disagreed completely on how I ought to be brought up. Father wanted a strict English childhood for me, and this is more or less what I got—nanny, governesses, supper on a tray in the nursery, dancing lessons, music lessons, skating lessons, art lessons . . .

Mother had the idea that she wanted me trained by a circus performer, that it would give me grace and coordination and self-assurance, but Father was horrified. I wish Mother had had her way. However, I did have Mrs. O.

Mrs. O. Nanny: odd, obsolete, un-American idea. But Mrs. O is worth a book in herself, as are so many of the other people in this tale. She's English, a Liverpudlian, and her family for generations had belonged to the highest order of English servants—and there is nothing more rigid or more snobbish than the English-servant class system. It started to break down during World War I, and vanished during World War II. There are a few nannies left, but not many. Mine is ninety-one this summer, still completely *compos mentis,* and passionately concerned with all the doings of my family. She has clucked with me many times about Mother's decline, and somehow she always manages to phone me on a day when things have been particularly difficult, and by the end of the conversation we are both laughing.

She was born Mary McKenna and came to the New World when she was fifteen, to spend a summer on Prince Edward Island taking care of four small children. At summer's end she went to visit one of her aunts, who was housekeeper for a wealthy family on Park Avenue; the enormous house is still in existence, now a club. There were four in the family, and forty on the staff, which included gardeners, coachmen, and outdoor laborers. The staff ate dinner at noon, around a long table below stairs, having a "joint" each day, bowls of potatoes, vegetables, salad. They were well fed, if hard-worked. The family dined at night. One of the daughters of the family, Miss Amy, fourteen, was blind as a result of scarlet fever. She was spoiled and demanding. Young Mary McKenna's aunt suggested that Mary take Miss Amy for a walk. When Miss Amy began to be difficult, not wanting to walk, whining, wanting to go home, Mary said, "My aunt said that you are supposed to walk for an hour, doctor's orders."

Miss Amy said, "I won't."

Mary said, "You will."

Miss Amy said, "I'll lie down in the street."

Mary said, "Go ahead, for all the good it will do you." It was the first time anybody had crossed Miss Amy since her blindness.

They walked for a full hour, and when they got home Miss Amy said to her mother, "I want Mary."

So Mary McKenna, barely older than blind Miss Amy, became a lady's maid. The next day the family left for a trip abroad, and Mary sat at the captain's table with Miss Amy, to help her. When the family went to Paris they arrived earlier than expected, and the floor of the hotel which was usually reserved for their use had not yet been emptied, so the servants were sent, just for one night, up to the top of the hotel, under the eaves.

Mary McKenna announced to one of the others, "I've never slept in a place like this before, and I'm not going to begin now." So she went looking for some way to summon help and express her displeasure. At one end of the attic she saw a series of brass bells, took a broomstick and began whacking away at them, making a considerable din. It was not until firemen came rushing upstairs with hoses and hatchets that she knew which bells she had rung.

However, she had made her point. She did not sleep in the attic.

With Miss Amy she traveled all over Europe, went to formal dinner parties, to the opera, to the theatre; because of Miss Amy's blindness she saw far more of the above-stairs world than would most lady's maids.

Then she met and married John O'Connell, whose brother is still remembered in Ireland as one of the great fighters of the Irish revolution. They had three daughters, and then the O'Connell family fell on hard times, and in order to help feed and clothe the children she went back to work, and the only work she could get was as a charwoman—the lowest rung of the English-servant caste system. It was a humiliation to her that few could understand.

She worked on Wall Street cleaning offices at night. My godfather often worked late and got to talking with this rather unusual cleaning woman, and once when his wife was having a large party and needed extra help, he asked Mrs. O'Connell if she could come to their house and help out. My parents were at that party, and later Mother phoned to find out who the splendid extra helper had been, and if she would come help at a party Mother and Father were giving.

When she arrived at our apartment, Mother smiled and said, "I don't even know your name."

"My name is Mrs. O'Connell, but I expect you will want to call me Mary."

"I'd be delighted to call you Mrs. O'Connell," Mother said, and that was the beginning of a friendship between the two women, and my nanny's entrance into my life. I was only a baby, and when I began to talk I called her "O," and a little later Mrs. O, and Mrs. O she has remained, and there are many people who don't know her by any other name. Wherever she is, she brings laughter, and a sense of fun, although her life, after she left Miss Amy, was full of pain and tragedy.

Until arthritis prevented travel, she spent several weeks with us three or four times a year, and I treasure a small snapshot of Mother and Mrs. O sitting on the sofa, side by side, nattering away. They share many of the same memories—of operas all over Europe, of singers; Mrs. O refers casually to Madam Melba, Jean de Reszke, Chaliapin. If Mother knew the people above-stairs, so did Mrs. O, and from the point of view of below-stairs, so she was able to tell Mother all kinds of little titbits she'd never have heard otherwise. She also enjoyed telling stories on herself, such as the time she was sent out to buy pâté de foie gras; when she reached the grocer she couldn't remember the French words, "but it sounds like Paddy Fogarty." The closest she has ever come to being vulgar is when she says, "Ah, well, I must go and shed a tear for Ireland," and heads for the bathroom.

She thought my father a prince, and treated him accordingly. She loves to tell of one summer when Mother and I were out of the city and Father was preparing to sail to Europe on an assignment. He couldn't find some things he needed, and knew that Mrs. O would know where they were. She didn't have a phone, so he sent her a telegram: COME AT ONCE.

She came, and there he was, she said, sitting

alone at the dining table, eating scrambled eggs by candlelight.

She also liked to tell of the times she met him on the street, when he would stand leaning on his cane and passing the time of day, "as though he didn't have anything better to do."

She was deeply religious, in a quiet way, and sometimes when she had a special concern on her mind, she would take me to church with her. She also thought—quite rightly—that I was overprotected, and took me on my first subway rides. She didn't like the fact that Mother would allow no sugar in my breakfast oatmeal; Mother always tasted the oatmeal to make sure no softhearted member of the household had sugared it; Mrs. O got around that by putting the sugar in the bottom of the porringer, and the oatmeal on top of it, and stirring it in after the porridge had been tasted, and Mother never knew, until we told her a few years ago, why I would always eat my oatmeal for Mrs. O. For I never told of the subway rides, or the visits to church, or the sugar in the cereal, or the little packets of butterscotch in the park; all I knew then and all I know now is that Mrs. O never taught me anything but good.

I used to say to her, "Will you help me take care of my children when I grow up?" And she would remind me of this on her visits to us.

When *A Night to Remember,* about the sinking of the *Titanic,* was on television, she sat and watched and rocked and clucked; she knew most of the guests from Miss Amy's family; the captain had been to the house many a time for dinner, and the young Mary would go to the ship bearing the invitation;

some of the crew she knew this way, and some from family and acquaintances in Liverpool; the movie seemed to have been filmed especially for her, and all of us watching it with her were far more moved by it than if we had not been seeing it through her eyes.

She was probably the most normal part of my childhood, and I will always be grateful for her. I think I realized that I was a subject of disagreement between my parents, and yet I managed to think that both of them were always right, and I'm sure Mrs. O had something to do with this. When I was asked by playmates which of my parents I loved best, I answered truthfully that I loved them both best. Maybe it was because I saw far less of them than the average American child sees of his parents; certainly a great deal less than my children saw of me. Mother was never very strong, and after she lost a little boy, at seven months—he lived a few days—it took her a long time to get her strength back. There were many times when she was in bed for weeks, with a white-uniformed nurse bossing the household.

The beginning of my life coincided with an end to my father's old way of life. Before the war he had been a foreign correspondent, traveling all over the world, often taking Mother with him. The dose of mustard gas in the trenches so damaged his lungs that it was necessary for him to live a quieter life than he had been used to. During my childhood he wrote mostly short stories, detective fiction, movies, plays. He had an office in the Flatiron Building, and he slept late and wrote late. Until his lungs took us abroad, to the Alps, when I was twelve, I don't think I ever ate at the table with my parents except on Sunday, and then, Mother said, "You didn't know what to say to us." I preferred eating alone off a tray, with a book propped on my lap. This may explain why the entire family eating together, around the table, is so important to me.

2

DURING THE EARLY YEARS of my parents' marriage, Father was music and theatre critic for the old New York *Evening Sun,* and he knew and loved opera; he belonged to the Opera Club, which meant that he was free to use the club box at the Metropolitan Opera House whenever he felt like it, and often, toward the end of a meal, he would say to Mother, "I think I'll just go down to the Met and catch the last act of *Boris.*"

I must have been around eight when Father decided that it was time for me to go to the opera. On one Saturday a month the men of the Opera Club were free to bring a lady, so I was taken to a matinee of *Madame Butterfly.* I listened and watched in fascination, absorbed by the music and the exotic story, but I was totally unprepared for this fairy tale not to have a happy ending. I went back to the apartment in a state of shock. When Father asked me if I had enjoyed the opera I replied that I had, and I told neither of my parents my pain at being drawn into the Butterfly's anguish.

Thinking that the first opera had been successful, Father next took me to *Pagliacci.* As soon as we had settled ourselves in our seats I turned to him: "Father, does this opera have an unhappy ending, too?" He told me that it did, and I began to cry, long before time for the curtain to go up. I cried and cried about the fate of Madame Butterfly, about the fate of Pagliacci, about all the unhappy endings I had been forced to realize were being played out all over the world; I cried until Father got up and took me home before the opera ever began.

It was a long time before he took me again.

Mother went with him to the Saturday matinees, and often in the evenings, too. I'm sure they were home more frequently than I remember, but I wasn't lonely. As a child, I enjoyed my solitary meals, my solitude in general, which, as I grew older, was interrupted by all the various lessons. Piano lessons I will be eternally grateful for. Dancing lessons were a horror; I was gauche on the ballroom floor as a child, and gauche I have remained. School was mostly something to be endured; I don't think I learned nearly as much from my formal education as from the books I read instead of doing homework, the daydreams which took me on exciting adventures in which I was intrepid and fearless, and graceful, the stories Mother told me, and the stories I wrote. It was in my solitudes that I had a hand in the making of the present Madeleine.

When I was a little girl—and older—I used to urge Mother to "tell me a story."

"A story about what?"

"About when you were a little girl."

The world of Mother's childhood, filled with playmates, most of them cousins, is a world I have never known. My children, spending their early years here in Crosswicks, came closer to the kind of childhood Mother had than I did. For the last decade or so, Mother has included reminiscences in her letters, so that I will have them to share with my children and grandchildren. A few years ago she dictated some accounts of the events of her childhood to a friend, but those typewritten pages lack the charm of her letters and conversations. She has not been able to write a letter for a long time. I will always miss the familiar blue paper with her beautiful handwriting.

The mother of my childhood and adolescence and very young womanhood existed for me solely as *mother,* and I suppose it is inescapable that for a long time we know our parents only as parents, that their separate identity as full persons in their own right unfolds only gradually, if at all.

I get a glimpse of what Mother was like as a very young woman when I think of her telling me about her first trip to Athens, before she was married. "I spent the first night on my knees by the window, worshipping the Parthenon."

It is not difficult for me to imagine that scene (and even easier, now that I have been to Athens myself), because it is completely in character.

My first actual memory of her is one of those complete, isolated visual glimpses, and is set in Cornish, New Hampshire, where my parents often spent the summer as part of the Saint-Gaudens Artists Colony. Homer Saint-Gaudens was one of my father's friends from the war, and he found the quiet and companionship a nourishing climate for his writing.

I was standing in a room surrounded by green—the house was aptly named Tree Tops—and Mother was showing me a small, white, embroidered dress, a dress for me, embroidered all around the hem with small red roosters, I thought it was beautiful. That dress, Mother told me later, was given to me by Madam Saint-Gaudens when I was two years old. What a strange, feminine first memory, especially for someone who has never had much of a flair for fashion! I have a feeling that there's more to it than that, that this gentle memory followed something hurtful—but I'll never know.

Although a writer of stories works constantly to train an observant and accurate memory, remembering is not necessarily a conscious act; it is often something which happens to me, rather than something I do. If I am ever tempted to take personal credit for remembering, all I need do is to think of the summer when I was eight or nine years old and Mother had cause to drag me with her around France. I must have driven her distracted, and she was convinced that I saw nothing.

However, my creative unconscious was storing up all that I saw, heard, smelled, tasted. Right now I have a completely sensory recollection of being sent on picnics in Brittany with three small boys, to get us out of the grownups' hair. For lunch we were given sour bread with sweet butter and bitter chocolate, and I still remember the marvelous combination of taste and texture. While we were eating we were surrounded with the sound and smell of ocean and wind, and our eyes were half closed against the brilliance of sky and sun, a blue and gold shimmer which comes only from sunlight on sea water.

Mother remembers a skinny, awkward, sulky little girl who saw nothing as she was dragged through châteaux and museums. Years later I amazed Mother as I described places and people of that summer in my first serious stories. What does—did—Mother remember of that summer; what was it like for her? I don't even know why we were there, without Father, and it is too late to ask her. I can only remember the summer as it was for me, not as it was for her.

When I needed memory of that summer for a story, my subconscious mind, with a porpoise-like flick, flipped it up out of the water for me. And I'm still young enough, active enough, that an enormous underwater treasure trove is available to me; I can swim for hours beneath the surface; or I can bring a shell, a piece of coral, up into the sunlight. Mother is like a sunken ship held at the bottom of the sea, with no choice as to the fishes who swim in and out of the interstices, the eels and turtles who make their homes in the remains.

When I remember the years in the apartment on Eighty-second Street, it is mostly the good things that I remember at home, and the bad at school. When I look at the apartment in my mind's eye, it is likely to be Christmas. This was the time when Father lifted from the physical pain in which he constantly lived, and the equally acute pain of knowing that his postwar work was not as successful as his earlier work. I did not understand my father's pain, but I knew that at Christmastime the apartment, instead of being heavy and dark, became sparkling and light as champagne, with Father sneaking home with an armload of presents, and writing stocking poems, and believing (I think) for a few weeks in a future in which there was hope.

On Twelfth Night he walked out of the house,

leaving Mother and Mrs. O to strip the tree, remove the holly from around the house, the sprig of mistletoe from the double doors to the dining room. And it was over for another year.

There was laughter at other times, too. One of Mother's favorite stories—and I know it only from her telling of it—was of an evening when Father went to the opera, and Mother, who wasn't feeling well, went to bed. After the opera was over, Father returned with a friend—my godfather—who went bounding into Mother's room, climbed into bed with her, and put his furled umbrella between them, announcing, "It's all right, Madeleine, this is Siegfried's sword."

I want to remember everything I can. Whenever Mother has a moment of clearness she is apt to reminisce, but these moments are becoming more and more rare. For most of it I must go deep-sea diving on my own.

3

I AM ONLY BEGINNING to realize how fragmented and uncoordinated I am. My left hand does not know what my right hand is doing. My heart tells me to go in one direction, and my mind another, and I do not know which to obey. I am furious with Mother for not being my mother, and I am filled with an aching tenderness I have never known before. There are rough waters below the surface of my consciousness, and strange, submarine winds. The submerged me is more aware of wild tides and undertows than the surface. One deep calls another, because of the noise of the water floods; all the waves and the storms are gone over me. And above the surface the brazen sun shines, heat shimmers on the hills, and the long fronds of the golden willow Mother planted ten or more years ago droop in the stillness.

I first became aware of the dichotomy between the daily world and the "real" world the year I was twelve. During my first years in New York as a solitary child, the world of my imagination and the world of daily life were not in conflict, because I had not grown up enough to see any difference between them. My real life was not in school but in my stories and my dreams. The people I lived with in books were far more real to me than my classmates. The Madeleine I wrote about in my stories was far more my real self than the self I took to school.

During that winter my father had one of his many bouts of pneumonia. If I was left to my own devices more than many children, it was because Mother's attention was focused on Father's injured lungs. He nearly died of that attack of pneumonia, and when he began, slowly, to recover, it was apparent that he could no longer live in the cities he loved—New York, London, Paris. He would have to be some place where the air is purer than in the city. During those Depression years it was less expensive for my parents to live abroad than in this country; Father's work went with him, with his small portable typewriter (it's still here, in the Tower) which had gone around the world with him on many assignments. But he was able to write little that winter of pneumonia and its aftermath. Money was short and for a few weeks Mother did the cooking—but only for a few weeks.

Fortunately, Mother had inherited her father's flair for business (even though she could not cook), so what investments she had been able to make before the Depression were not wiped out. Her first indication of financial talent came during the early years of her marriage. She had been downtown shopping and was returning home on the Fifth Avenue bus. Two men in dark business suits, bowler hats, and attaché cases sat in front of her, and she overheard them talking of a certain stock which could be bought for "practically nothing" and which was shortly going to increase immensely in value.

That evening she and Father went to a dinner

party in a large town house. After dinner a string quartet provided entertainment. Mother was seated behind a large potted palm, and by a man who was a stranger to her. "I was terribly shy, I felt completely out of place in all that elegance, and just to make conversation I mentioned the stock I had heard about that afternoon. He gave me a very funny look, and changed the conversation, and I thought I'd made some awful gaffe. But the next morning he telephoned me and said that I had startled him the night before, but he felt he ought to tell me that he was putting everything he owned into that stock. He offered to buy some for me, so I bought a hundred shares, which took what was a lot of money for us in those days. When I told your father, he was furious, so when my stock had doubled in price I sold fifty shares and paid him back. It more than doubled."

Mother seldom looked smug, and she did not when telling this story. The closest I have ever seen her come to looking smug was much later, when she told Hugh and me about going against all advice in buying some stock, and hitting the jackpot again. "I had the reputation of being able to put my hand down in the mud and come up with a piece of gold."

I, alas, have inherited none of this financial flair, and I certainly do not have what it takes to be a gambler. Once when my parents and I were in Avignon, Father gave me twenty-five centimes to put in one of the hotel gambling machines. I couldn't lose. Money kept pouring out. When I realized that the machine was broken, I took my ill-gotten gains to another machine and lost everything—except the original twenty-five centimes, which I kept.

Mother wasn't a coward about money, and it was

her financial acumen which kept things going during many lean periods.

The spring after Father's bout of pneumonia, Mother broke up the apartment where she and Father had lived for nearly twenty years, put some of their more treasured things in storage, and off we went into an indefinite future of searching for places where Father could breathe more easily.

We spent the first summer in the French Alps, above Lake Geneva. With my godfather and his family, which included the three boys I had picnicked with in Brittany, my parents rented an old château in Publier, a tiny village off the beaten track. It was found by accident: the real-estate agent had been showing us hideous modern villas which he considered more appropriate, and happened to mention the untenanted Château de Publier, and my parents had to argue him into taking them to see it.

There must have been a hundred rooms, most of which were left with sheets draped over the furniture. The kitchen had not changed since the Middle Ages, but the village girls who came to work for us had never cooked in any other way and would have disapproved of a modern kitchen. In the vast living room was a fireplace large enough to roast an ox, and a small, usable harmonium, which was my delight. Off the duchess's bedroom, in which my parents slept, was a small, octagonal chapel, with old, stained-glass windows, and a carved mahogany *prie-dieu* with a red velvet kneeler. The château actually had a bathroom, put in during the early days of plumbing. Under the tub was a firebox in which a fire had to be built in order to heat the water in the tub. I don't remember having a bath in it, and I probably never did. In all the bedrooms were large china pitchers and bowls, and most of our washing was done there in the old-fashioned way.

I was happy that summer because I lived completely in the world of the imagination—the only way I could escape being drawn into my parents' unhappiness. I wandered through the centuries, being the daughter of the château, Madeleine in the twelfth century, the fifteenth, the eighteenth. I wrote stories and poems, and I lived an interior life which protected me from the teasing of the three boys as well as from the world of the grownups.

It was during that summer that I was punished by my mother for the first time unjustly—at least, I felt it to be unjust. We had driven down to Lake Geneva to go swimming, and I had been allowed to go out by myself in a small sort of kayak, quite safe, since it was flat-bottomed. I paddled well out into the lake, lost, as usual, in reverie. It must have been a long dream, because when I turned my kayak around and paddled back to shore, everybody was furious with me, and I was punished because I had not come when I was called.

"I didn't hear anybody call," I told my mother. Nobody believed me, and it was probably not distance which kept me from hearing, but the depth of my concentration on my dream. My punishment was that I was not to read or write for twenty-four hours, which was the most terrible punishment possible to me, and I felt unjustly treated. At twelve I still stubbornly insisted on seeing my parents as Olympian, above earthly pain or problem. I'm not sure whether I did not realize what an unhappy summer it was for them, or whether I refused to realize. Father was having to face that never again could he live in the cities where he had the intellectual companionship he needed, the sharpening of wit against wit. Friends he had expected to stand by him were turning their backs, now that he was ill, now that his writing was not as successful as it had once been. Mother shared in both the suffering and the exile. The parents of the three boys were often away, and she had the responsibility for them, something she was not accustomed to. As I look back on it now, the fact that Mother and Father managed to keep the summer happy for me speaks of considerable nobility.

The medieval inconveniences of the château which were a delight to me must have been a daily irritation to my mother. It was an unusually hot summer, and there was no refrigeration. Friday was a special day because the fishman came through the village with his horse-drawn, high-smelling wagon, and the fish were kept passably fresh with ice. Mother bought not only fish for the evening meal but a small amount of ice—very small, just enough so that on Friday nights the grownups could have martinis before dinner. After dinner my special treat was to take a lump of sugar and dip it in Mother's or Father's demitasse, and then slowly let the warm, coffee-saturated lump dissolve in my mouth.

The substance of my days was as subterranean as the deepest of the cellars where the vegetables and eggs and milk were stored. This dream world ended abruptly on the day my parents took me away from the château and to boarding school. In my naïveté I hoped that the school would be a continuation of the dream. My first inkling that school was not going to be like a story came during the very first hour, when the matron, in crisp white uniform and even crisper accent, said, "If you have read boarding-school stories, Madaleen, forget them. School is not like that."

It was not. It was, at first, sheer hell. The term had started three days earlier, and I understand now that the decision to send me had been sudden and arbitrary, and had come after bitter quarreling. Mother wanted to take me with them higher into the Alps—for, even in Publier, Father found breathing difficult—and send me to the village school. Father felt that I would not get a proper education there, and that the French I would learn would be a questionable patois. I think also that he thought he was going to die sooner than he eventually did, and did not want me around, for both our sakes.

4

SO I WENT AWAY TO SCHOOL. Those first three days missed were disastrous. The other new girls had already found friends. I was completely alone, and the only American, to boot. The only other foreigners were Teri and Danusch Zogu, nieces of King Zog of Albania, and I have often wondered if they survived the terrors which came to their country. We bitterly resented the fact that they had a suite with a fireplace; the only other active fireplaces in the unheated building were in the infirmary and the headmistress's apartment.

But most terrible of all was that my imaginary world was ruthlessly wrested from me. Nothing was ever said about daydreams or the weaving of stories; daily life in school was set up so that there was no time and no place for the world of imagination. Our life was completely regimented from the moment we were roused to a bell, to the moment our lights were turned off to another bell. We had fifteen-minute bath "hours" twice a week, and anybody who dared stay in a lukewarm tub sixteen minutes was routed out by Matron. Bathrooms were constantly monitored, and a locked door was knocked on after two or three minutes. "Who is in there? What are you doing?"

Most of us had chilblains during the winter months. We used to sit in bed at night with tears running down our cheeks, rubbing Mentholatum into hands which were chapped raw and bleeding. Our diet would have provoked a riot in a present-day prison. I remember mostly watery potatoes, and suet pudding with one seed of raspberry jam as filling, so heavy we could feel it clonk into a cold lump in the pits of our stomachs as we swallowed.

It did not occur to me that there was any way out of this torture until another new girl wrote home asking her parents to take her away, and suggested to me that this was a perfectly possible way out for me, too. When her parents drove up and she left, I wrote to my mother and father in Chamonix, telling them of my misery, and asking them to come for me.

When Mother wrote saying that she and Father had talked my letter over, long and seriously, and that they were asking me to stay and to learn from my experiences, I did not realize how difficult it was for her to say no to me, or how right she was to do so. After a few weeks I did considerable adjusting. I was not happy, but neither was I unhappy. I learned to put on protective coloring in order to survive in an atmosphere which was alien; and I learned to concentrate. Because I was never alone, because (except after the lights-out bell) I was always surrounded by noise, I learned to shut out the sound of the school and listen to the story or poem I was writing when I should have been doing schoolwork. The result of this early lesson in concentration is that I can write anywhere, and I wrote my first novel on tour with a play, writing on trains, in dressing rooms, and in hotel bedrooms shared with three other girls.

Sending me away to school may have been an arbitrary decision on my parents' part, an end to their dispute about me and an answer to "What are we to do with her?" But I was irrevocably changed and shaped by the school and by my reaction to it. In the spring, when our chapped hands finally healed and we moved from heavy woolen underwear and scratchy serge gym tunics to Liberty cottons, we were given small garden plots to cultivate. We were assigned partners; I was Number 97 in the school (even then, the process of un-Naming had begun); 97 on my clothes, my desk, my napkin cubbyhole, my shelf in the classroom, my locker in the common room; and my partner was 96. We were allowed to bring the produce of our gardens in for tea, so almost everybody planted tomatoes and lettuce and radishes and cress. 96 and I planted poppies. Nothing but poppies.

It was possible when I was twelve to be considerably more naïve and innocent about drugs than it is today. All we knew was that opium comes from poppies, and we knew this because our illicit reading included Bulldog Drummond and Fu Manchu. From these paperback books, which we kept hidden in our blazer pockets to read when we got sent from the classroom, we learned that opium produces beautiful dreams. So 96 and I ate poppy-seed sandwiches, poppy-flower sandwiches, poppy-leaf sandwiches, and went to bed every night with our dream books and flashlights under our pillows. My dream book has been lost somewhere, but I am still grateful for it. I soon learned that poppy sandwiches weren't needed to induce dreams, but they did serve to give me an awareness that the waking world isn't all there is.

If we had been allowed more time for daytime dreaming, for excursions into the world of the imagination, if we had been allowed time for what George MacDonald calls *holy idleness,* we would not have had to depend on our nighttime dreams. But holy idleness would not have been tolerated in that school, and any attempt to search for it was considered wicked and immoral. "What! Daydreaming again, Madaleen? You'll never get anywhere that way."

Where did Matron want me to go? Our civilization was rushing toward the devastation of the Second World War; the clouds were visible on the horizon, and my parents saw them, even if Matron didn't; and yet in school we were being taught to live in a climate where it was assumed that man is in control of the universe, and that he is capable of understanding and solving all problems by his own effort and virtue.

What 96 and I were doing with our dream books was instinctively rejecting this false illusion, refusing to think that our whole self is limited to that very small fragment of self which we can know, control, and manipulate; that very small fragment of self over which we have power.

At that time the two worlds lay side by side for me; the imaginary world in which I had been moving was just behind me; I was still fending off the limited, finite world of school with stolen moments of dreaming and writing. I had yet to learn that the two worlds should not be separated. Growing up is a journey into integration. Separation is disaster.

Look at my mother this summer. She is lost

somewhere in the subterranean self; she cannot come up into the light of the day. She is no longer the integrated person I have loved and admired, but a dark shard broken and splintered.

❧

Bedtime has always been a time for me when the above-water world of the mind and the undersea world of the imagination, the world of the intellect and the world of intuition, have come close. In boarding-school days I treasured bedtime not only because it was my only time of privacy but because it was daydreaming time, and I was angry if I became sleepy too soon. In my Swiss school the dormitory windows opened out toward Lake Geneva, facing the always snow-crested mountains of France on the other side. When I was fortunate enough to have my bed by the window I could lie and look at one of the most spectacular views in the world; the view itself was a consciousness expander, and disciplined my daydreams.

Long before the language of Freud and Jung became part of our everyday vocabulary, Emerson wrote, "I catch myself philosophising more abstractly in the night or morning. I make the truest observations and distinctions then, when the will is yet wholly asleep and the mind works like a machine without friction. I am conscious of having, in my sleep, transcended the limits of the individual, and made observations and carried on conversations which in my waking hours I can neither recall nor appreciate. As if in sleep our individual fell into the infinite mind, and at the moment of awakening we found ourselves on the confines of the latter."

Our dream books were not so foolish.

I still treasure the time before sleep comes, when I move into the shallows before plunging down into deep waters; and the minutes before I surface into daylight and the routine of the day, when I swim slowly up from sleep and dreams, still partly in that strange, underwater world where I know things which my conscious mind is not able to comprehend.

5

THIS IS A STORY with a double helix. I am trying to write about a particular summer, the summer that will always be for me the great-grandmother's. I am trying to take a new look at my mother's life and world, and I find that I can do this only subjectively. I can look objectively at Mother's life only during the years before I was born, before my own remembering begins, when I did not know her; and even then my objectivity is slanted by selectivity, my own, hers, and that of friends and relatives who told me stories which for some reason Mother had omitted from her repertoire. I learned a good deal of family scandal one Crosswicks summer when I overheard Mother talking to my mother-in-law.

But there attempts at objectivity fall apart, and biology makes me subjective, and this is the other strand of the intertwined helix, my very subjective response to this woman who is, for me, always and irrevocably, first, Mother; and second, her own Madeleine.

❧

Change is a basic law of life, and when change stops, death comes. But change is not automatically good; it can be for the worse as well as for the better. If I need any proof that all change is not good, all it takes is five minutes with Mother. She tries to break things, throw things, fights moving anywhere, cries, "No, no, no, no," over and over; often does not know where she is, or who we are; or, if she does know who, then *whether* we are. "Are you real? You aren't made up?" There's something to learn from this strange, senile madness about the nature of reality.

Am I making Mother up as I remember her? Am I overcompensating, as the jargon would have it? No matter. What I remember is a woman who was fully alive, who enjoyed new tastes, sounds, adventures.

That year when I was twelve and she and Father spent the winter in Chamonix, Mother was not happy. The rented villa was as inconvenient as the château, and cold. At night she had to cover the washbasins with quilts so that the pipes would not crack. The ink froze, and had to be thawed in the morning. She told me, when I was grown, that the mountains closed in on her. The winter was snowy and cloudy, the village enclosed in grey. Only rarely would she wake up in the morning to clear skies and Mont Blanc on fire from sunlight.

But what I remember, from the Christmas holidays I spent with my parents, was the coziness of the villa, which she had somehow made into a home, despite hideous wallpaper with designs that looked like spiders, chairs of brilliant green plush and sagging springs.

I remember, too, the new glimpse of my parents which followed our separation. Nothing would ever be the same again; they would never be the same. I went up to their bedroom one afternoon looking for Mother, and saw her flung out on the bed in an abandoned position of grief, and I backed out in horror. I do not think she knew that I had seen her. And I began to notice that Father was drinking more than was good for him, but I did not understand the reason why.

During this summer of the great-grandmother, I am aware again of my father. His portrait is over the mantelpiece, a charming, impressionist piece done long before I was born, painted in an apple orchard in Brittany. The occasion for the portrait was a swashbuckling felt hat and a red tie he'd bought in Cairo. Mother hates the portrait, which I love. The man who looks at us is vital, full of *joie de vivre;* and he belongs to another, more gracious but equally brutal world; this portrait could not have been painted after that world ended, with World War I. I never knew the man in the portrait; I knew only the man whose world had been demolished in that war, and who took eighteen years to die.

Mother would say, "Your father and Gilbert White used to take a pitcher of martinis and go out to the apple orchard while Gilbert painted; you can see the martinis in your father's eyes." I can't. This is hindsight on Mother's part. I see only the handsome, blond young man full of pleasure, not because of martinis but because he'd just completed an exciting assignment; because the apple orchard was beautiful; because he was full of *élan vital* and *amour-propre.* (Odd: when I try to express joy I turn to the French words, and to German for pain: *Angst; Sturm und Drang; Weltschmerz.* It was my parents' wanderings which gave me these words; I gained many valuable things because of their troubles.)

I began to know Father after his death. During

his life I never heard him complain, so I did not understand about his pain until later. Nor did I understand that alcohol, which had been a pleasure in an apple orchard in Brittany, became a painkiller, and occasionally an abused painkiller. As I look back now, I am amazed that it was so seldom abused. My own struggles with pain, with defeat, help me to know my father and to love him, not as I had loved him before that winter in Chamonix, as a small child looking up to an impossible god, but with a love which begins to struggle toward *ousia.*

That month in Chamonix was an ambiguous one for me. When I could, I reacted as a child, but I was being forced into growing up. I wanted to balance the pain of school with comfort, safety, changelessness, but I found pain, discovery, change. I listened to Mother playing Bach on a barely playable upright piano, and I watched her play solitaire. Because she could not understand Father, neither could I, and I was drawn into her unhappiness.

And yet that Christmas was one of our loveliest. All the decorations on the small tree were homemade. We still hang on our Christmas tree each year a small silver chain made of little beads of tinfoil, rolled from the paper in Father's packages of Sphinx cigarettes. We cut pictures out of the English illustrated magazines to replace the horrors on the wall which came with the rented villa. My presents were the very books I had asked for, plus colored pencils and a fresh box of water colors and a new notebook with a marbleized cover. What we ate for Christmas dinner I don't remember; all we ate that winter, it seemed, was rabbit, which was plentiful and cheap;

and Berthe, the eighteen-year-old girl Mother had brought with her from Publier (for, even that austere winter, she managed to have help), cooked rabbit every conceivable way. And a few inconceivable, Father would add. We also ate hearts of palm; for some reason the village grocer had an overabundance of this delicacy, and needed to unload it. Berthe bargained with him and came home triumphantly with string bags bulging with cans.

On New Year's Eve I was allowed, for the first time, to stay up with my parents until midnight. I remember only one thing about that milestone: while the village clock was striking twelve, Father opened his small new engagement diary for the year, and we all signed our names in it. It was Father's way of saying *yes* to Mother and to me and to the new year, no matter what it might bring. It would have been much easier for him to withdraw from it, as he occasionally withdrew from the pain with whiskey, but he refused to withdraw, and I knew this without understanding it in the least, and was grateful as I added my signature to Mother's and his.

My father's name: Charles Wadsworth Camp. When I wrote my first published stories and had to decide on a writing name, it was with a wrench that I decided to use my baptismal name, Madeleine L'Engle.

Mother said, "It's as though you're rejecting your father."

"I'm not!" And I reminded her that it had taken her a year to decide whether or not she could go through life as Mrs. Camp. Add to this the fact that many publishers at that time were friends and contemporaries of my father, and I wanted to be a writer on my own. And I'm sure that Father would have been the first to agree that Madeleine L'Engle is a more felicitous name for a writer than Madeleine Camp.

When I married Hugh I was all set to switch to Madeleine Franklin, but my publishers said that I had already made a good start under L'Engle, and Hugh agreed.

My first novel was a success, and it was not until we were living in Crosswicks and I began to receive what seemed an interminable stream of rejection slips (for nearly a decade I could sell nothing I wrote) that I began to understand what the failure of his last years must have been like for Father.

Long after his death Mother told me that one day she went into his room to call him in for lunch. It was at the very end of his life, when they were living in my great-grandmother's cottage at the beach. Father's bedroom and office was a corner room overlooking ocean and dunes, with the sound of the surf and the wind in the palms ever present. He was sitting at his desk, and when she came up to him he stopped typing and handed her several pages.

Mother did not know how to be dishonest, and she sometimes infuriated Father by falling asleep in the evening while he read his day's work to her. Now, slowly and carefully, she read what he gave her, and then she said, "Charles, this is *good.*"

His eyes filled. "I can still write, can't I?"

I cannot set this down without tears coming to my own eyes.

My father's name was his, and I will always honor it. A name is an important thing, and I did not decide on mine lightly. Perhaps it was Father's affirming signature on that cold New Year's Eve in France which underlined forever the importance of a name.

During those weeks in Chamonix we went everywhere on skis, the simplest method of moving on the snow-packed streets, and I learned more complex skiing on the slopes above the villa. We spent a memorable day on the Mer de Glace, and those hours of walking over a sea of ice were a revelation of a cold and unearthly beauty I had never before seen. My own vision was deepened because I saw the beauty through the eyes of my parents; their wholehearted response took us all beyond the pain and confusion which were ever present in the villa. One night we rode for an hour in a horse-drawn sleigh, snow beneath us, moonlight and starlight above us, the horse's mane streaming coldly in the wind, while we were kept warm under fur robes. Father hardly coughed at all; Mother relaxed and enjoyed the beauty and the speed. I moved back into my dream world during that ride, not as an escape, but as a respite; I did not try to take the fairy tale with me back into the villa.

And I remember a summer evening somewhere in France. We went to a tiny, one-ring circus. The ring was enclosed with a fence as insubstantial as chicken wire, and when a shabby lion came roaring out of his cage I grabbed my parents' hands in an ecstasy of terror, fully expecting the old beast to leap over the flimsy barrier. I think that this memory must precede the winter in Chamonix, though I have lost its chronology, because I still felt complete security sitting between Mother and Father. After Chamonix I would have known that there are lions more powerful than my parents.

The lions I feared during my childhood were the

lions of war. I was born after the Armistice, and yet the specter of another war after the War to End Wars was always with me, not only because of Father's coughing, but because of my own terror of war; I am not sure where this terror came from, but it was always with me. Quite often I would anxiously ask one parent or the other, "Is there going to be another war?"

They paid me the honor of not trying to comfort me with false promises—though I doubt if they foresaw the enormity of change to come in the ways of waging war.

Father's war was not like our wars today. In his war the enemy still had a face. When you killed, you killed a man, not a town or village of people you did not know, had never seen, would never see.

Once, a good many years after the war, my parents were eating dinner in a Spanish inn, and suddenly Father got up from the table in great excitement and rushed across the dining room to a man who, in his turn, was hurrying to greet Father. The two men embraced warmly, and Father brought his friend over to the table to meet Mother: the man was a German; he had been an officer in the Kaiser's army; he and Father had fought against each other at the front. It is difficult to understand such an incident today. These two "enemies" were genuinely happy to see each other; they had shared an extraordinary experience; they respected and honored each other. I wonder if that can happen today, even at the higher levels of combat.

I was in boarding school in Charleston, South Carolina, when we heard the news that Mussolini had taken troops into Ethiopia. I will never forget the leap of terror in my stomach, followed by a dull ache of acceptance: this was the beginning of the war about which I had been having nightmares since I was a small child.

It was a worse war than Father's war, yes, and has continued to be so, through the bombings of England, Europe, Korea, Vietnam, the Middle East.

But there is one small note of optimism: the results of mustard gas were considered so terrible by so many people that it was not used during World War II, nor has it been used since—though we have used worse things. English children during the bombings went to school carrying gas masks, but they did not need to put them on.

We have seen the terrible results of the atom bomb. We know how bad it is. Perhaps it, like mustard gas, will never be used again? It may be a faint hope, but it is a hope.

6

HERE IN CROSSWICKS I listen to Bion and his friends soberly and painfully discussing the involvement of the United States in Vietnam, Laos, Cambodia. For Bion this is not only the summer of the transition between high school and college, the summer of watching his grandmother become daily less human; he must also decide whether or not he can honestly register as a conscientious objector. One of his friends is a Quaker, and his position is absolute. Bion's is more difficult. He totally disapproves of American involvement in Vietnam; but can he say, truthfully, that under no conditions would he ever fight? Given the circumstances of his Grandfather Charles's war, what would he have done? Is there such a thing as a just war? Could the war with Hitler have been avoided? There are no easy answers.

A little less than a year ago, at the end of the summer, the night before he went back to school for his final year, he announced to us, "I'm not playing football this year."

"Why, Bion?"

"It's a blood game, and I don't want to have anything to do with it."

"Well, it's completely between you and the school. If you think you can handle it, go ahead."

Bion is pushing 6′5″, weighs two hundred pounds, and was expected to be a useful member of the football team. There was a good deal of pressure put on him to play, but he was adamant. They said, "But you play goalie in ice hockey. That's much more dangerous than football." "I'm not worried about the danger. The way we play hockey, it isn't murder."

I think he expected to be ostracized. Instead, he was given both respect and support. He went with the team to the games, and one Saturday at an away-from-school game, one of the boys on the other team was hurt—not badly it seemed, and nobody was particularly worried.

That evening many of the boys were in their coffee house when the headmaster came in to tell them that the boy on the opposing team had died. "The chapel will be open all night," he said, "for anybody who wants to use it." There wasn't a boy in the school who didn't go into the chapel, just to sit, to think about death, if not to pray.

During this decisive period Bion came home for a weekend and announced to us that he had become a vegetarian. "I may not keep this up, but it's the way I feel now." We respected the fact that it was a response to his thinking about war and peace, and whenever he was home I cooked quantities of extra vegetables.

He finally decided that he could not say that under no circumstances would he fight, ever. His two little nieces may have played a part in that decision. I think there's no question that he would fight to defend them. He also feels deeply about Crosswicks and the land around it; he was born here; here are his roots. If his land were attacked he would fight to defend it; his land: Crosswicks: his country.

His is only one of many reactions to the violence that is increasing all over the world. How strangely contradictory we are: we condone slaughter of villages or towns in our various wars, and yet we will do anything to keep a hospitalized body alive, a body whose central nervous system has been destroyed—a kind of reverse euthanasia. I do not want this for my mother. To be a body without *ousia* was what she dreaded most. She is not in physical pain, though everything within me cries out that she is in spiritual pain.

We all in the Crosswicks household, to the limits of our capacity, share the pain. And we are learning daily lessons in interdependence. I lost my unquestioning dependence on my parents that winter in Chamonix. I am still learning to move into interdependence.

Because of the girls who make up the great-grandmother's retinue, because of the understanding and compassion of the entire household, there is still laughter in the rooms. Yet there are times when for no logical reason I feel an almost unbearable sense of isolation. Not only am I divided in myself, my underwater and above-water selves separated, but I feel wrenched away from everybody around me. This is part of being human, this knowing that we are all part of one another, inextricably involved; and at the same time alone, irrevocably alone.

Alone, and yet interdependent. Much of my

training has been against accepting this paradox, my good Anglo-Saxon boarding-school training. Stand on your own feet. Do it yourself. It's your own business. Don't bother anybody else with it. Take in your belt a notch, pull up your boot straps, and go it alone.

Not bad advice in many ways. Who wants a clinging vine? But there's more to it than that. Mother fought dependency as long as she could, but that's a different thing from interdependency. She lived alone during the winters far longer than I thought was safe for her, and yet I would not take away the dignity of risk until she herself was ready—which was not until the intestinal resection, when she was nearly eighty-eight. When I think of the varied climates and conditions in which Mother lived, I marvel at her ability to adapt. Would I too be able to take with equanimity the enormity of change through which she strode?

7

DURING MY last year in school—the school in Charleston, South Carolina—my parents were living at the beach in North Florida in the drafty old cottage built by my great-grandmother. In late October, Father made his annual pilgrimage to New York and Princeton, and my mother took a trip driving around North Carolina with Aunt Dee—one of my godmothers. Mother arrived home a day or so before Father and drove into town to meet Father's train. "When I saw him get off the train," she said, "I knew he was dying."

That night she wrote to me. The next day I was busy with some project and did not even check the mailboxes, until a friend came bustling up, being the bearer of good news, "Hey, Madeleine, there's a letter in your cubbyhole."

It was a brief note in which Mother told me that Father was in the hospital with pneumonia, and asked me to write to him. She ended the letter, "Pray for him, and for me, too."

I had always been a bad letter writer. I managed to get off one cursory note every Sunday, in which I told almost nothing of what was going on without or within. I didn't really know what or how to write to Father, but I copied out three poems I had written that week, and sent them to him, knowing that they would arrive too late. This knowing was not prescience; I had been watching him die for years, and I knew that he could not last through another attack of pneumonia.

The next afternoon the headmistress sent for me and told me that my father was very ill and that I was to take the evening train home. I was not surprised at her summons, although when it came I felt shaky and cold. Two of the teachers drove me to the station and stayed with me until I got on the train. In those days it was a four-hour trip, and I had taken *Jane Eyre* with me to read, but I could not read. Whether or not I believe in God I have always prayed, and I prayed then, though I did not ask God to make my father get well. I prayed to the rhythm of the wheels, "Please, God, do whatever is best. For Father, for Mother. Please do whatever is best, whatever is best, is best. Please, Father. Please, God, do whatever is best for Father."

My two godmothers met me, Aunt Dee and Cousin Mary, my mother's close friends since childhood. I asked how Father was and they evaded answering me, and so I knew the answer. It wasn't until we were nearly at our destination that one of them told me that Father had died that morning, and that we weren't going all the way to the beach, but to the house of a cousin.

I don't know why Father's funeral was in this house, rather than in church. It seems very strange to me now, and I cannot ask Mother to explain. I remember feeling embarrassed as I kissed Mother, and then even more embarrassed when I was told, in the manner of those days, to go in and look at Father.

He was lying in state in the library. I asked to go in alone, and stood in front of the coffin and looked at him. His face was peaceful and alien, and my father was not there. I closed my eyes, and then I was able to see him a little better.

I remember nothing about the funeral, but I remember the trip to the cemetery, and the canvas canopy put up to shield us from the heat of the subtropical sun, still apt to be oppressive in late October, and that I thought the canopy out of place and would have liked to move out from under it. I remember staying that night in Aunt Dee's great, dark house, and that Mother and I talked about trivial things in a completely calm way. For some reason we talked about toothpaste, but we were really talking about Father.

I do not know whether or not the Church was any comfort to Mother at the time of Father's death. It was not to me. The words of the burial service were strengthening, but not the unctuous men at the graveside.

If the churches and synagogues didn't condone the mortuary mentality, funerals would not be the travesties they so often are. One rainy day when I stood at a favorite cousin's graveside, huddled with family and friends under umbrellas while the rain slanted in from the east and trickled down our necks, I was repelled by the phony carpet of green grass thrown over the pile of earth waiting at the open grave. I think we grossly underestimate the capacity for realism in the mourner.

What would I have wanted for Father, what will I want for Mother if she predeceases me? She may not; at the birthday party in the spring a cousin said, "Don't worry about your mother. She's going to bury us all."

Alan's grandmother, my mother's contemporary, as a young woman in an English village was a "layer-outer." And I would want this, to have a human being (so this is what I think of morticians!) prepare my parents' bodies for burial. Alan's grandmother knew each body she touched, as we know each other in our village.

I would have been happier if my father's body had been buried from the house at the beach, his last home. If Mother should die while she is with us in Crosswicks, I would like to have her body prepared at home, and then to have the four traditional candles placed, one at each corner of her bed, and to take turns watching and honoring her earthly frame during the night, and thinking soberly about death, her death, mine, and being free to do some grieving, some weeping over the mortal remains of my birth-giver.

Many professional religion-mongers I have encountered are so terrified of and so disbelieving about the Resurrection that it is no wonder that they condone cozy coffins and fake grass. My own theology is very shaky here, and I find most strength in the writings of the early Byzantine Fathers, men who, like us, were living at a time of radical change. They have far more in common with the world we are living in today than thinkers of a generation ago. The early Fathers were living, as we are, in the breaking apart of a great civilization. The Roman world was shattering like an ice floe in the spring. Nothing was ever going to be the same again. So the *ousia* of things, all that which was true, is true, and will be true, had the same kind of importance for them that it does for us. I turn to these golden-tongued writers (long turned to dust) with a sense of familiarity, of talking with known and well-loved friends. They are our contemporaries, and I understand their language, even if I myself falter when trying to speak it.

They are more aware of the wild freedom of creation than we tend to be. They probe beyond limited sensory evidence in an effort to glimpse *ousia*—the *ousia* of a parent, or a small green frog on a rock—to glimpse it, not with limited human eyesight and comprehension, but with the whole of themselves, that whole which encompasses the unknown worlds beneath the waters and beyond the stars.

I am often afraid of this world. It would be simpler to restrict myself to the things I can hear and see and touch, to the things I can prove, to the things I can control.

My senior year at boarding school I thought I was pretty well in control of my world; I was editor of the literary magazine, played leading roles in the school plays; I was, for the first time, a success with my peers, and this success was heady wine. And then Father's death pushed me right out of the slippery world of human control, and I had no choice but to try to open myself to the darkness and horror in order to search for a hope of finding a possible all-rightness on the other side.

My father was dead. What was all right?

When Gregory of Nyssa's brilliant sister, Macrina, was on her deathbed, she sent for Gregory, and brother and sister talked throughout the night. He held her hand and told her, "The Resurrection will bring about the restoration of our human nature in its original form." This is strong and difficult language. Gregory and Macrina never doubted the Resurrection, but they thought of it neither as a vague continuing in unending time, much as we are in mortal life, nor as an awakening of the dead body from the grave, old bones and flesh reassembling themselves to make the same flawed body that died. Rather, they thought of it as a radical change of all that we have come to think of as ourselves.

I had not encountered a theology as wild and strong as Gregory's when Father died. I had to struggle alone, and all I knew was that Father's death caused me to ask questions for which I could find no answer, and I was living in a world which believed that all questions are answerable. I, too, believe that all questions are answerable, but not in scientific terms, or in the language of provable fact.

Mother sent me back to school almost immediately. And I wanted to go. I understood only dimly what the loss of a husband who had been lover, friend, companion for thirty-odd years would mean to this woman who was my mother.

Back in Charleston I went at the first opportunity out into the grounds and climbed up into the ancient live oak tree which was my favorite writing and reading place, and coldly and calmly recorded the fact of Father's death in my journal. It was a long time before I was able to cry—nearly three years; and it was falling in love for the first time which freed the tears.

That last year at boarding school I was working on a series of boarding-school stories; it was the world I knew best and instinct told me that I should write out of experience. During the spring term I tried to write about Father's death, and I wrote it almost exactly as it had happened—for my protagonist was a tall, clumsy, nearsighted girl—and the story had a certain amount of verisimilitude, but I knew that I had not yet really written it, that I had not got it out where I could face it. Occasionally I would talk to someone about death—not the girls at school, or the one or two teachers I really trusted, but young men.

The only good I could find in Father's death was that my coming-out party was canceled. But a cousin was being launched and Mother insisted that I go to some of the parties. "Your father would have wanted you to. And I want you to."

I don't think she realized quite how agonizing these dances were to me, the stranger in a tightly knit group of young people who had known each other all their lives, and who were fluent in an agreed-upon set of social mores which were completely unfamiliar to me. Dates were arranged for me, and I'm sure the young men whose parents had coerced them into calling for me dreaded the evenings as much as I did. I was as tall as an adolescent as I am now, and most of my dancing partners seemed to be at least a foot shorter, and leaned their heads against my breast as we danced—or as I tripped over their feet. I was hopeless in the social world, and had none of the highly cultivated charm of my Southern cousins.

One cousin, trying to be helpful, drew up a list of ten questions for me to ask my dancing partners. I was always extremely myopic, contact lenses had not yet become general, and pride forbade me to wear my glasses on a date or at a dance. But there was one dance where I had more partners than usual, and spent less time in the ladies' room pretending to put on make-up, desperately thinking up excuses to keep me off the dance floor, and I was feeling quite pleased with myself, and was prepared to tell my cousin how well her questions were working, when my partner said, "Hey, honey, what's your line? You've already asked me these questions three times before."

I couldn't very well tell him that I was so short-sighted that I hadn't recognized him, so I said, "You haven't really answered them properly."

"You really want to know?"

"Of course, or I wouldn't have kept asking."

We became friends after a fashion, and talked about the primitive pubic rites of the coming-out parties, and felt sophisticated and above it all.

And I learned that when a boy talked to me about God, and death, he was likely to give me a good-night kiss, even if I put on my glasses at the movies.

Through my partner at that dance I met a brilliant, unhappy young man who later became a physicist, and I remember one conversation we had, a conversation which I reproduced, almost verbatim, in a different setting, in my first novel, where I struggled to write the *ousia* of Father's death in depicting the death of the protagonist's mother.

The original conversation was held at the beach, at night. Instead of taking me to the movies as planned, Yandell (named, in the Southern manner, after his mother's family name) said, "I feel like talking," and then drove in complete silence the forty-five miles to the beach. We climbed up onto a high dune and listened to the grave rolling of the waves, and the gentle hishing of the tall sea oats, and Yandell told me that he had a heart murmur and probably wouldn't live for more than a few years. He asked, "How old was your father?"

"Fifty-seven."

"That's a lifetime. At least he had a lifetime."

"It's not very old." I come from a long-lived family.

He shrugged, and we lay back on the dune and looked at the stars. "Did you see him after he was dead?"

"Yes."

"I haven't ever seen a dead body. What did he look like?"

"He looked—he didn't look real. He wasn't there."

"Where do you think he was, then?"

Something in his tone of voice made me sit up. "You don't think he's anywhere, do you?"

"I didn't say that."

"But do you? Do you believe that my father *is,* now—himself, somewhere, actively living, *himself?*"

He picked a long sea oat and began slowly stripping it and dropping the little pieces on the sand, sea oat and sand blending together. "What you believe about things like that is just your own personal opinion, isn't it?"

"You don't think he is. You think he's just nothing, don't you?"

"You're grown up enough to see through all this coming-out zug. But if you want to go on with the tribal superstition thinking your father's more than worm fodder, that's up to you."

I was both angry and frightened. I stood up, and sand slid under my feet. "Yandell, I saw him when he was dead. I saw Father, and it just wasn't Father. It's like looking at a photograph; it looks like the person, but the person isn't there. Father wasn't there, not what's really Father. And if he wasn't there, he's got to be somewhere."

The caustic note had gone from Yandell's voice, and he spoke slowly and calmly. "But what's a soul without a body, without senses? Can you imagine existing, being yourself, if you couldn't see? Or hear? Or feel? And after all, we think with our brains. How could you be you without your cerebral cortex?"

I was so angry that I nearly burst into tears, but they wouldn't have been the right kind of tears. "It's idiotic," I said, "it's crazy. If you die and then you're just nothing, there isn't any point to anything. Why do we live at all if we die and stop being? Father wasn't ready to be stopped. Nobody's ready to be stopped. We don't have *time* to be ready to be stopped. It's all crazy."

"Don't think the idea of extinction appeals to me," Yandell drawled.

I had put on my glasses so that I could see the stars. Now I took them off and the sky became nothing but a dark curtain. I waved my glasses at him. "Look at my glasses. I can't even see that there are any stars in the sky without them, but it's not the glasses that are doing the seeing, it's me, Madeleine. I don't think Father's eyes are seeing now, but *he* is. And maybe his brain isn't thinking, but a brain's just something to think through, the way my glasses are something to see through."

"Calm down," Yandell said. "Let's go walk on the beach and go wading."

One cold winter's night in Crosswicks, many years later, while I was putting the children to bed, my daughter Maria turned to me and said,

"Grandma says my mother got all burned up." True: Liz was cremated. But to the seven-year-old child this insensitive sentence from Liz's mother meant the entire loss of Liz. That day I had given away some of Maria's outgrown dresses, and I reminded her of it, and that we had bought her some new clothes. And I said, "You'd outgrown those old clothes, and you don't need them any more. And now you have clothes which fit you better. Well, if a human parent can get new clothes for you when you outgrow your old ones, God can provide us with new bodies when we outgrow the ones we have now."

I can't begin to guess with what kind of body he may have outfitted Liz or my father, or will outfit my mother. However, I have a feeling that it would be completely unrecognizable to our human eyes. At least the analogy I used for the seven-year-old child was one step away from the thinking of the Middle Ages, where there are records of the burial of a Crusader home from the wars with only one leg; at his death a leg was cut off one of his peasants, on the theory that the Crusader would have more need of two legs in heaven than the peasant.

That medieval horror would have pleased Yandell—who outgrew his heart murmur and is alive and flourishing. And I admit that my thinking isn't a great deal less primitive than that of the Middle Ages. The main progress is that I do not attempt to give an answer to an unanswerable question, but I do ask the question. And it does not upset me unduly that Paul's vision of a "spiritual body" is a scientific impossibility, and can be glimpsed only in poetry and paradox.

When I got back to boarding school after the holidays, Yandell's words obviously remained in my underwater mind, and I worked out a scheme of things which still seems valid to me. It was a logical analogy for one who had spent so many years in boarding schools, because it included thinking of our present lives as being something like nursery school, and to complete the growth of our souls we would need to go all the way through school and college and a great deal further.

I sat, during a free weekend afternoon, out in my favorite live oak tree, and thought of the stars over the ocean during my painful conversation with Yandell, and that all of those stars were suns, and that many of these suns had planets, and that surely the planet earth is not the only planet in the universe to have sentient life. And then I thought that perhaps there might be a planet where nobody has eyes; everybody would get on perfectly well; other senses would take over. But nobody on that planet could possibly conceive of what sight could be like, even if they were told about it. Something as important and glorious as sight couldn't be understood at all.

So then I thought that maybe when we die we might go to another planet, and there we might have a new sense, one just as important as sight, or even more important, but which we couldn't conceive of now any more than we could conceive of sight if we didn't know about it. And then when we'd finished on that planet we'd go on to another planet and develop and grow and learn even more, and it might well take millions of planets before we'd have been taught enough to be ready for heaven.

I haven't gone much further than that adolescent analogy, and even then I knew that it was no more than analogy. But I did feel, and passionately, that it wasn't fair of God to give us brains enough to ask the ultimate questions if he didn't intend to teach us the answers.

8

It would have been easy, after my father's death, for Mother's love to become grasping and demanding. The environment in which she lived encouraged it. But Mother deliberately opened her hands and let me go. Many of my Southern relatives expected me to stay home and take care of my delicate mother; however, during vacation times Mother carefully pointed out shriveled female cousins who had spent most of a lifetime caring for an aged parent "while life passed by, so now that Cousin Isabella has finally shuffled off her mortal coil, her daughter has been sucked dry and it's too late for living."

Some of my shriveled female cousins had just cause to think of "Mother"—or "Father"—as devourer. But I worry about people who assume that *all* mothers are bloodsuckers. The womb is a place of dark, warm protection only for a term; as soon as the baby is able to bear the light of day the womb contracts and expels him, loosens him, frees him.

A friend of mine spoke of college freshmen as people wandering around with the umbilical cord in one hand, looking for some place to plug it in. Often the mother has cut the umbilical cord long before the child is willing to let go, and yet the child blames the mother.

When I was sent, so abruptly, to boarding school, the umbilical cord got cut, ready or not, and Mother had no intention of reattaching it. Thanks to her clarity of vision, I was able to go to college free of guilt.

We had spent a happy summer in England and France, visiting relatives. We came back to New York just a few days before college, and then off I went on the train, heading north into New England, and Mother returned to the South.

I did not abandon or forget Mother. I did not understand consciously that she was sacrificing something in sending me away, but I think I must have instinctively felt more than I knew, because from the time of Father's death and on, until she could no longer read letters, I wrote her at least a postcard every day. It became a simple part of the day's routine and took only a few minutes.

I had a good four years of college, by which I mean that I did a great deal of growing up, and a lot of this growing was extremely painful. I cut far too many classes, wrote dozens of short stories, and managed to get an excellent education despite myself.

After college I did not even consider yielding to family pressure and returning South to "take care of your mother," but went to New York to live my own life and work in the theatre, which I considered the best possible school for a writer. The daily epistles, and weekly (collect) phone calls continued, but I was free to become my own Madeleine.

My mother was birth-giver, not devourer, and I hope I have learned from her.

What is time like for Léna and Charlotte? It is longer than for the rest of the household. It is so long that it comes close to breaking time and becoming part of eternity. But it is not that way for the very old. Time unravels, rather than knits up. It is as erratic as nightmare.

My mother's senility has drawn her through the keyhole of reality and into the world of nightmare on the other side. Her fears are nightmare fears, like those of one who has just woken out of a bad dream and cannot get back into the "real" world. Her real world is gone. She is trapped in nightmare and all our loving cannot get her out.

The pressures of time can sometimes weigh very heavily, but this weight is bearable. One of the greatest deprivations of senility is the loss of a sense of time. Time is indeed out of joint. An old man or woman in a "home" or hospital may say tearfully to a visitor, "My children haven't been to see me. They've forgotten me. They brought me here and abandoned me. They don't care any more." The children's last visit may have been the day before, but to the old man or woman it was so long ago that it has been forgotten. Times stretches like old, worn-out elastic. What happens if it is stretched till it breaks?

Two years ago when it became clear that reading my daily epistles was burden, rather than pleasure, to Mother, the phone calls increased from once a week to twice a week, and finally to almost every day. Last winter I was frequently rebuked for not having called for so long. "I called day before yesterday, Mother." "You didn't. You haven't called for at least two weeks " Occasionally I would get a call or a letter from a friend or relative in the South: "Why haven't you called your mother?"

It is thin-skinned of me to be upset. For several years I have known that when Mother returns South after the summer she will tell everybody who will listen that I haven't fed her properly. Sometimes I will have this reported to me with an understanding smile. "She looks absolutely marvelous. The summer did her a world of good." Sometimes her complaints will be accepted at their face value, and I am a cruel daughter.

It's a very American trait, this wanting people to think well of us. It's a young want, and I am ashamed of it in myself. I am *not* always a good daughter, even though my lacks are in areas different from her complaints. Haven't I learned yet that the desire to be perfect is always disastrous and, at the least, loses me in the mire of false guilt?

Perfectionism is imprisoning. As long as I demand it, in myself or anybody else, I am not free, and all my life—fifty-two this summer—I've believed that freedom is important, that, despite all our misuse and abuse of it, freedom is what makes us a little lower than the angels, crowned with glory and honor, according to the psalmist; how like a god, according to Shakespeare; freedom to remember, to share, to dream, to accept irrationality and paradox is what makes us human animals.

Where is my freedom this summer? I can go no farther from the house than I can walk, because chancy vision no longer allows me to drive. The responsibility of my mother, of the large household, of the kitchen stove, would seem to deny me a great deal of freedom, and yet my freedom is still up to me. Because I have entered willingly into this time, I do not feel that my freedom has been taken away.

But there are times in life when human freedom

is denied us, and not only in prisons and concentration camps. I was once in an extremity of pain and knew that I was close to death. I was fighting hard to live, for my husband, our small children, for myself and all that I still wanted to do and be, for all the books I hoped to write. And then I knew that unless the pain was relieved I was not alive, that death was better than the body continuing in this kind of impossible pain which had me in its brutal control. When they took me to the operating room I barely had strength to move my lips, "I love you," to Hugh. As for prayer, I could do no more than say, "Please," over and over, "please," to the doctors, to Hugh, to God . . .

My freedom was entirely out of my hands.

Once I heard a "good" woman ask if the victims of concentration camps did not find consolation in prayer, and I was shocked by the question. It was directed to me, and I answered, fumblingly, that they were probably in that dark realm which is beyond the comfort of conscious prayer, and I likened it to extreme physical pain. There have been times when I have given way to the heart's pain, too, and again have been outside freedom. We *can* be unmade, un-personed, all freedom taken away. That we do this to each other is one of the great shames of our civilization. It is not people, but atherosclerosis, which is taking freedom away from my mother.

But I still have some freedom, even when I go alone in the starlight down the lane to weep, with the dogs pressing anxiously about my legs; not much freedom, but some, that little luminous pearl which is daily misunderstood and misused, but which makes life worth living instead of a dirty cosmic joke.

9

ONCE WHEN MOTHER and I were in New York, during a college vacation, we had lunch together in a pleasant downtown restaurant before going to the theatre, and I remember, with the same clarity with which I remember the little embroidered dress, that I leaned across the table and said, "Oh, Mother, it's such *fun* to be with you!" And it was. We enjoyed things together, the theatre, museums, music, food, conversation.

When I was pregnant with Josephine I told Mother, "All I could possibly hope for with my children is that they love me as much as I love you."

Josephine, when she was five or six years old, lightened my heart one evening when she flung her arms around me and said, "Oh, Mama, you're so *exciting!*" What more glorious compliment could a child give a parent? My parents were exciting to me, but their lives were far more glamorous than mine. When Jo made that lovely, spontaneous remark I felt anything but exciting; I was in the midst of a difficult decade of literary rejection, of struggling with small children and a large house; and that remark of Jo's restored my faith in myself, both as a writer and as a mother. Even though I knew I might never again be published; even though I could not see any end to the physical struggle and perpetual fatigue,

Josephine helped heal doubt. It is a risky business to hope, but my daughter gave me the courage to take the risk.

I wonder if I ever, unknowingly, gave my mother like courage? I am well aware of all the things I have done which have distressed her, but perhaps simply the fact that I have always loved her may sometimes have helped.

A story should be something like the earth, a blazing fire at the core, but cool and green on the outside. And that is not a bad description of my mother. Her exterior was so reserved that it was a long time before I realized that there were flames beneath the surface. She was, in my presence at least, an undemonstrative woman, undemonstrative with me, with my father, with everybody. What Mother and Father were like alone I don't know, especially what they were like in the early years of their marriage, when they were young, when Father's health was unimpaired. I never knew the young couple who traveled all over the world at any and every opportunity in all sorts of conditions; who, when they were in New York, ran with a pack of artists of all kinds, as well as with a small, close-knit group of intimate friends. It is difficult today to understand the deep and abiding friendships among men who had survived the First World War together, but the inner circle of friends was composed of three or four men who had fought side by side with Father, and of their wives.

As I look back to the New York years, there seem to have been countless parties. Mother told me, "Your father could walk cold sober into a dead party, and in five minutes everybody was having a good time. He was like champagne."

I had only glimpses of this effervescent man in my own life; I understand far more of his *ousia* now than I did while he was alive. Sometimes in restaurants he embarrassed Mother—and so me—by being what she thought was rude and overdemanding. The strange thing was that the waiter or headwaiter she thought he had insulted, instead of being insulted, thought Father was marvelous, and though this always happened, Mother could never get accustomed to it. When he went into a fine restaurant he demanded fine food and fine service, and when he did not get them, he let people know, and in no uncertain terms. After one hotel dinner somewhere in France when Father had been his most imperious, and Mother less understanding than she might have been, she apologized by telling me of a time when they had gone to a restaurant in Paris where Father had made what she considered a scene; several years later they returned to the same restaurant; the maître d'hôtel greeted Father by name, as an honored client; and the headwaiter served them exactly the same meal Father had finally managed to get years before. Even during his last years my father had a quality about him that was not easy to forget.

I remember my parents coming, night after night, to kiss me good night and goodbye in their evening clothes, Father often with his top hat, looking like a duke, I thought.

Why do I remember with such pain going to sit in Mother's lap one day when she had someone in for tea, and she pushed me down, gently, and said in her quiet, just slightly Southern voice, "You're too old to sit on my lap now."

How old was I? I don't remember, but not, I think, very old. Perhaps that is why I let my children make their own decisions as to when they were too old for lap-sitting.

I told this to Mother, once, perhaps in defense of my lap-sitting policy. She did not remember the incident, and I think that this is part of the human predicament, that most of us are not aware of the small things we do—or don't do—that cause pain which is never forgotten.

One memory of being pushed away from Mother's lap? That's all? One memory of being punished unjustly?

Oh, we had our clashes, Mother and I, we're both temperamental enough for that. During school or college holidays I wanted to write or read or paint or play the piano when Mother wanted me to be social. I could not be for her the gracious and graceful young woman she dreamed of. Nevertheless, I often heard her say that one belief in which she never faltered was that I had been born for a special purpose, and this belief led her to set up impossible standards for me, and when I failed to live up to them she would scold. It sounds as though her expectations put an intolerable burden on me, but somehow she managed to keep them from doing so, and it has been only in the past years that she has referred to them frequently.

"I know you were born for something special."

This would have been more of a burden to me if it weren't part of my mythology that this is true of every child. The fairy godmother or guardian angel bestows on each infant a unique gift, a gift to which the child will be responsible: a gift of healing; a gift for growing green things; a gift for painting, for cooking, for cleaning; a gift for loving. It is part of the human condition that we do not always recognize our gifts; the clown wants to play Hamlet.

While Mother was still herself, I never wondered overmuch about this. Whether or not my gift is with words, which she hoped it was, I will never know. In any case, writing is something I'm stuck with, and I realized this when I first hurt her with something I had written—hurt Mother, not Father, because I did not begin to probe the past until after he died. Until then my writing was poetry, which wrote me, rather than vice versa, and stories of wish-fulfillment and wild and improbable fantasy. But the year that Father died, writing began to push me.

One has to listen to a talent, and whether the talent is great or small makes no difference. As I fumbled for truth in my stories I was not consciously aware of responsibility to them, I only knew I had to write what was asking to be written. So I wrote story after story of a man and woman and their young daughter wandering across Europe. Many weaknesses which I did not consciously acknowledge as being part of the make-up of my parents were clearly delineated in these stories, although when I was writing I had no idea how coldly accurate they were. I didn't even fully realize that I was writing about my parents. All I knew was that I thought they were good stories, and I showed them to Mother for appreciation.

I was appalled when she cried. My reserved

mother seldom permitted herself the indulgence of showing emotion, and I had made her cry. I had no idea how close the stories had hit home. I did not know that in the stories I knew more than I knew.

I was full of sorrow that I had hurt her. But I continued to write stories and I continued to show them to her, and occasionally made her laugh instead of cry; and even when I hurt her, she could move from her first, instinctive, "I don't see how you could write that!" to, "But it's a good story. It's very good. Keep on."

Ever since I have been old enough to drink coffee, we have had our morning coffee together whenever she has been in Crosswicks, or whenever I've been with her in the South, and these long kaffeeklatsches have strengthened our friendship. It frightens me this summer that I can no longer talk to her about her fears. When I went to be with her at the time of the intestinal operation, she was still able to put her fears into words, and to receive comfort from my presence, my hand in hers, if not from anything I tried to say.

Several times she reached out to me. "I know that even if I get through this operation I don't have very long to live, and I don't know where I'm going. I feel hypocritical when I go to church, because I can't say the Creed."

"Why not?"

"I don't believe it any more."

"Did you ever?"

"I don't know."

"Mother, you can't understand the Creed like

your Baedecker guide to Athens. It's in the language of poetry. It's trying to talk about things that can't be pinned down by words, and it has to try to break words apart and thrust beyond them."

"But I'm supposed to believe—"

"No, you're not," I say firmly, holding her hand. "It's all right." Dimly I realize that she is caught in the pre-World War I philosophy, that same philosophy 96 and I rebelled against, that world of human perfectibility and control.

She says, "I can't take Communion because I'm not worthy."

"Oh, Mother, if we had to wait till we were worthy, no one could ever take Communion."

I certainly could not. But Mother isn't the only one to talk to me like this, nor is it only her generation. Students have talked to me in the same words. Someone is still teaching theological hogwash. What is this restrictive thing they feel they have to conform to or be hypocritical? If I have to conform to provable literalism I not only rebel, I propose immediate revolution. How do I make more than a fumbling attempt to explain that faith is not legislated, that it is not a small box which works twenty-four hours a day? If I "believe" for two minutes once every month or so, I'm doing well.

The only God worth believing in is neither my pal in the house next door nor an old gentleman shut up cozily in a coffin where he can't hurt me. I can try to be simple with him, but not vulgar. He is the *mysterium tremendens et fascinans;* he is free, and he understands the *ousia* of this frightened old child of his. No wonder I can't believe in him very often!

That morning, sitting with Mother over coffee, I read the Collect for the day and made a beautiful mistake, reading, "Almighty and merciful God, of whose only gift it cometh that thy faithful people do unto thee true and *laughable* service." Surely *laughable* is a more appropriate word than *laudable,* for even with the prodding and companionship of the Holy Spirit the best we can do must provoke much merriment among the angels.

I get glimmers of the bad nineteenth-century teaching which has made Mother remove God from the realm of mystery and beauty and glory, but why do people half my age think that they don't have faith unless their faith is small and comprehensible and like a good old plastic Jesus?

Mother sips her coffee and says, "I know you were born for something special." Ouch. "I'm glad you go to church."

I sigh. On Sunday I had gone to Mother's church, and I was not happy there. I went mostly for her sake, and my mind kept turning off, turning away from the service, worrying about the upcoming operation which I knew might well be fatal; worrying about the family at home; being anything but worshipful and prayerful. But I did have one creative kind of thought which I tried to share with Mother.

"You know what, Mother, lots of people, ages varying from fifteenish to seventyish, talk to me about the books they could write, if only . . . The reason they don't ever get around to writing the books is usually, in the young, that they have to wait for inspiration, and you know perfectly well that if an artist of any kind sits around waiting for inspiration he'll have a very small body of work. Inspiration usually comes during work, rather than before it. With people around my age the excuse is usually that they don't have time, and you know perfectly well that if a writer waited until there was time, nothing would ever get written."

She nods. "Yes, but what does that have to do with the Creed?"

"Wait. I've talked with a lot of people who think that any kind of formal prayer, like that gorgeous Collect we just read, is wrong, that we should wait for inspiration to pray."

"Well?"

"I don't think it works that way. I prayed very badly in church yesterday. I often pray badly when I try to say my prayers at home. But if I stop going to church, no matter how mad church makes me, if I stop praying at home, no matter how futile it sometimes seems, then 'real' prayer is never going to come. It's—well, it's something like playing the piano. You know what happens when I don't have the time to play the piano for a week or so—my technique falls apart."

"It certainly does. It's never very good."

"Okay, but at least the very small amount of technique I have is needed when I try to play the C minor Toccata and Fugue."

She nods. "You're beginning to play it quite nicely."

"Well, then, do you think prayer is any easier than the fugue? If I don't struggle to pray regularly, both privately and corporately, if I insist on waiting for inspiration on the dry days, or making sure I have the time, then prayer will be as impossible to me as the C minor Fugue without work."

"Where on earth do you think of these things?"

"But does it make any sense to you, Mother?"

"I don't know. Maybe. Yes, I think it does, a little. I knew you were born for a reason."

"Writing. And just to be your daughter. More coffee?"

10

THAT IS one of the good memories. It is typical of many of our breakfast conversations; in the early morning over coffee I am apt to pontificate, which is one reason Hugh and I never eat breakfast together except on vacation, and then I try not to talk until he has had two cups of coffee.

The good memories far outweigh the painful ones. In recent years Mother's and my morning talks have often stretched until nearly time for lunch, and we talk about everything under the sun—literature, politics, as well as theology. We have often disagreed, and argued excitedly, but never, on these large subjects, angrily.

Now there is no longer the possibility of disagreement. Our long discussions are over. The girls bring her in to the living room and she sits on the little sofa for the hour before dinner. She is no longer interested in sipping her drink, or eating her "blotters," as she used to call the crackers for hors d'oeuvres. She is humped over; she does not even notice that the stockings are wrinkled on her still shapely legs.

Our conversation wreathes about her like smoke; she notices it only to brush it away. It is only with an effort of will that I can remember the evenings when she joined in all our discussions. Peter is talking about parallel universes, that all possibilities are somewhere, in some galaxy or other, being played out. She does not hear, she who would once have loved to join in the speculation.

In the old days over our morning coffee I enjoyed sharing my science-fiction imaginings; we discussed theories of the creation of the universe, side by side with local politics. We talked about fashions, food, the development of the children. I sounded off, after Grandfather's death, about funeral practices.

"How can those ghouls blackmail people?" I asked vehemently. *"Do you want to buy a coffin that isn't as nice a coffin as so-and-so bought?*—as though the price of a coffin could be a measure of love."

I considered that family pressure had made her spend too much on Grandfather's. "Mother, haven't we lost sight of how to honor people's bodies?"

She put me right on the spot. "How do we?"

"Not with expensive, cozy coffins, as though Grandfather could *feel* the quilted silk and the little pillow. He's dead. He's lifeless clay and he's going to turn to dust." Then, afraid I had hurt her, even though a hundred years had made a travesty of my mother's father, I said, "Anyhow, I'm glad the funeral service is exactly the same for the Queen of England as for an unknown pauper. Otherwise I haven't any answer." I looked across the room at Mother's chest of drawers, on which stood a small mahogany chest with a swinging mirror; it had gone across the United States with Mado and William L'Engle, her grandparents. It had suffered from exposure to inclement weather, and now from the wet wind from the St. Johns River; some of the beautiful veneer was chipped and buckled. She followed my gaze. I said, "Maybe we honor a human body in somewhat the same way you honor Mado's little chest. Oh, Mother, I don't know. I don't know how we honor Grandfather's—or anybody else's—body, except by giving it to God."

She pushed me further. "How do we do that?"

I drank some tepid coffee and chewed a piece of cold bacon and sighed. "Maybe by accepting that God knows more than we do, and that he really does count the hairs of all our heads. That's what I want to believe, but all I can do is fumble. I just think the people who know all the answers are all wrong."

Here my intellect, my above-water self, and my intuitive, below-water self, are in conflict; but I have learned from painful experience that although intuition must not ignore or discard the intellect, it can often take me further; and I am more apt to find the truth of love in the world which 96 and I were searching for with our poppy sandwiches than in the reasonable world of the adults who thought they were in control of it all.

Mother said, "It's almost eleven o'clock. We ought to get dressed."

But too much coffee has the effect of making me talk. "You know what, Mother, one place we've gone wrong is in thinking of death as failure."

"As success, then?" she asked dryly.

I shook my head. "When Liz and Arthur died, in worldly terms they failed Maria, failed her totally, didn't they?" I did not mention Father. Mother didn't answer, so finally I said, "Oh, Mother, if we aren't free to admit failure we aren't free at all. I don't understand it; it's a mystery; but I know that unexpected good things have come to me out of what I thought was failure."

"Like what?"

"Oh—if *A Wrinkle in Time* had been sold right away instead of going from publisher to publisher all that awful long time, it might have been published and just quietly died."

Mother agreed. "That's true. I don't think I understand anything you've been saying, but I think it's true." Then we turned our talk back to Grandfather. We were glad the 101-year-old body had finally given up the ghost, but we knew we would miss the brilliant being he once was.

We got up and dressed.

"Who is going with me when I die?" Grandfather had asked. Mother can no longer ask anything. She can voice nothing but fear.

I tell a friend that I hope for Mother's death, and he is shocked; he sees it as a failure in my love toward her.

Perhaps it is. I don't know.

When I try to honor her body as it is now, and as it will be when she dies, I can go no further than when I was an adolescent, talking to Yandell, or when I was sounding off to Mother over morning coffee. Intuition holds me in the direction of Gregory of Nyssa's words to Macrina, and this is enough to keep love alive in my heart.

I love my mother, not as a prisoner of atherosclerosis, but as a person; and I must love her enough to accept her as she is, now, for as long as this dwindling may take; and I must love her enough, when the time comes, to let her go into a new birth, a new life of which I can know nothing, and which I cannot prove; a new life which may not be; but of which I have had enough intimations so that I cannot discount its possibility, no matter how difficult such a possibility is for the intellect.

I will try to share one of these occurrences which I call intimations. I cannot call upon them to come; I have no control of them whatsoever; they usually happen during Emerson's vulnerable moments between sleeping and waking, or when I am so tired that my conscious mind lets down its barriers.

This past spring, after Mother's ninetieth-birthday party, I flew back to England with Josephine and Alan and the babies, to spend a week with them in Lincoln, and a few days in London seeing friends. The flight from New York to London seemed unusually long. We were served lunch immediately after departure, and then nothing else at all, not even tea, though we did manage to get some milk for the little ones.

Because of the time gap it was eleven o'clock at night when we arrived in London, and it took us over an hour to pick up the car in which we were to make the five-hour drive to Lincoln. We were very hungry, but all restaurants and coffee shops were closed. Alan said we would try to find an all-night truckers' café on the way.

I sat in the back of the small car, suitcases piled up beside me, Charlotte on my lap. I was very tired, not because of the trip but because the birthday festivities had been exhausting, emotionally and spiritually even more than physically. Josephine and I began to sing to the little girls, trying to lull them into sleep, taking turns in singing the old nursery and folk songs, many of which had come to us from my mother.

Then, suddenly, the world unfolded, and I moved into an indescribable place of many dimensions where colors were more brilliant and more varied than those of the everyday world. The unfolding continued; everything deepened and opened, and I glimpsed relationships in which the truth of love was fully revealed.

It was ineffably glorious, and then it became frightening because I knew that unless I returned to the self which was still singing to the sleeping baby it would be—at the least—madness, and for Josephine and Alan's sake I had to come back from the radiance.

Alan pulled the car into the parking lot of an open café. I was able to get out and carry Charlotte in, to sit down at the table, to nod assent as Alan ordered bacon and eggs and tea, but I was still not back. I talked through cold lips in what must have been a normal fashion, because neither Josephine nor Alan asked if anything was wrong, and I drank cup after cup of strong English tea until gradually the vastness of the deeper world faded away, and I was back within myself again, talking to my children and eating bacon and eggs.

Was this no more than hallucination caused by fatigue and hunger? That may have been part of it, but only part. I offer no explanation for this vision of something far more beautiful and strange than any of the great beauties I have seen on earth. I only know that it happened to me, and I am grateful.

But I do not need frequent visions to be fortified by the truth of love, my mother's love for me, a love which I cannot conceive of as having any end, no matter how much it is trapped within her this summer.

Her concern is something I have automatically assumed, as a matter of fact. It was nearly impossible for me to hide anything from her. When I phoned her when I wasn't feeling well, or was unhappy about something and chatted, perfectly naturally (I thought), she would say, "What's the matter? Something's wrong." Cool, undemonstrative, reserved, yes, but tender. Gentle and soft but with a core of steel.

Now, during my adult years, if I wake up in the night and am frightened, as occasionally happens, I control my terror by myself. Hugh needs his sleep; I am grown up now and I do not wake him to hold and comfort me—although simply his presence, the rhythmic sound of his breathing, helps push me through the fear.

But when I was a child and we were living on Eighty-second Street I could call for my mother when I woke up and was frightened, and she would come to me and sit on the side of my bed and stroke my forehead until I was quiet and ready to go back to sleep. When I was a little older I would slip out of bed and across the hall and into her room and get in bed with her, knowing she would never reject me. She would put her arms around me and hold me close and say, "It's all right," and then I could go to sleep.

I sleep this summer because I am too tired to stay awake. If I wake up during the night my ears strain to hear Mother, although out in the Tower I cannot hear her. Sometimes in the afternoon I go out to the hammock, which is strung between two ancient apple trees halfway to the brook, and out of earshot of the house. Sometimes there, swaying gently, and surrounded by green leaf patterns shifting against the sky, I can relax into peace.

III

The Mother I Did Not Know

1

"Tell me a story, mother," I used to demand in the very early morning in the days on Eighty-second Street when I climbed into bed with her before breakfast.

Often she would reply,

> *"I'll tell you a story*
> *About Jack a Minory,*
> *And now my story's begun:*
> *I'll tell you another*
> *About Jack and his brother,*
> *And now my story's done."*

"No, no, Mother! A real story!"

"What kind of a story?"

"A story about you when you were a little girl."

She was born in 1881, my mother, just after the end of the Civil War, with the memory of it still fresh, and she said, "with the memory bitter indeed." Carpetbaggers had arrived in full force, and the old Southern families, most of whom had lost fathers and brothers and homes and money, resented what she termed the "Northern interlopers."

She called her paternal grandparents Amma and

Ampa. "They came from the West, and although they came from real Southern stock, they were Western in their speech and mannerisms." She loved them dearly, particularly Ampa, with whom she often used to spend the night, sleeping with him in a great four-poster bed.

All this talk of being in bed with parents and grandparents: it reminds me that while I was in college I wrote a story about a very small girl who woke up on the morning of her birthday and ran joyfully into her parents' room to climb into bed with them and open her presents there in the warmth and safety of their presence. The professor announced to me that the reason the child wanted to get into bed with her mother and father was that she wanted to sleep with them sexually, a sort of combination Oedipus-Electra complex. I dropped the course without credit. But the remark has obviously left its mark in that I think of it each time I write about getting into bed with Mother, or Mother sleeping with Ampa. Such a thing could—and should—be spontaneous and completely innocent of Freudian connotation, and it is a sad commentary on today's climate that I hesitate in the telling.

Amma and Ampa came to the South from Kansas not long after the war, because Amma's migraine headaches were relieved in the more temperate climate. In Kansas they "had lived the life of pioneers and had no time for social graces. But when they came South, the fact that they were of Southern ancestry was in their favor with the Southerners." And my grandfather, Mother's Papa, was an attractive young man, and a skilled athlete. "He met a good many of the young men around town and was soon taken into their crowd."

Because I grew up in another time and another world, all that she told me was as strange as a fairy tale, and I never tired hearing about it. In an apartment in the city of New York, Mother showed me the vast plains of Kansas. On a hot summer city night she told me of the far greater heat of the Kansas plains at a time when few trees had been planted. "Amma used to take a big watering can on hot summer nights and go about the house sprinkling the sheets until the beds were cool enough to lie down on." Suddenly New York seemed cooler.

"Papa grew up on horseback," Mother told me. "He was given a Kickapoo pony when he was a very little boy."

"What's that?"

"It's an Indian pony, and it has the tribal mark of the Kickapoos—each ear split about two inches. His next pony was a Texas cow pony which was his constant companion. Papa went out with him every evening to bring the cows home. Every household kept one or two cows, and they were all turned out together in the morning to feed on the rich prairie grass. Sometimes Papa would find them two or three miles away, and he said that all he had to do was to get his pony to 'start cutting our cows,' and then he could put his reins down and the pony would do the rest." He was a crack shot and provided much of the food for the table.

Grandfather was living in Scotland during our years on Eighty-second Street, but he came to America once a year, and before one visit Mother told me a story about something that happened to him in Kansas when he was nine years old. While he was whittling, his knife slipped and stabbed him in the right leg. At each beat of his heart, blood spurted from the wound. He called for his father, who checked the bleeding temporarily by pressure. The only available doctor did not know the difference between a vein and an artery, and simply bandaged the leg. As the blood continued to ooze through the bandage, he stopped it by putting a piece of wood on the bandage immediately over the puncture.

Grandfather was left in this condition for nearly two weeks, by which time his entire leg below the bandage was swollen and had turned black. Then a Civil War surgeon happened through the little township of Hiawatha, saw the injured boy, and told his father that the only chance to save his life was to amputate the leg next to the body. Ampa asked if there was no possible way by which the leg could be saved. The surgeon said there was one chance in a hundred that if he ligatured the artery it would hold, but he thought the leg was so diseased that he could not advise it. Ampa said, "I will take the chance."

The operation was performed on the kitchen table, and was successful. It was a long time before Grandfather could walk again, but that did not hold him down; he went everywhere on horseback with his closest friend, the son of the chief of the Sauks and Foxes. When he learned to walk again, it was like an Indian, lithe and silent, one foot directly in front of the other, and he walked that way all his life. This rigorous training made him both an athlete and a beautiful dancer. He overcame his lameness so completely that when he went to the University of Kansas he won the track meet.

Years later he was persuaded to return to Kansas

for his sixtieth college reunion. He was at that time an active and virile man who would have been taken for someone in his late fifties. When he stepped off the train, one of his boyhood friends was there to meet him, and hobbled along the platform, leaning on a cane. In an old, squeaky voice he quavered, "Hello, Bion."

Grandfather took one look at this old man, bounded back up the steps of the train, and never turned back.

He had come a long way from the Kansas plains of his boyhood; he was a highly sophisticated and cultivated man; going back was in all ways an impossibility.

I could never write a biographical book about Grandfather. He was a self-made man and a great man, and like all such he had the weaknesses which were the other side of his strength. He hurt people, and the telling of his story would hurt more people. Perhaps he will come to me sometime as a character in a novel, as my parents have already done, more than once. In a fiction the events of his life would have to be toned down, because they are too incredible. In a story, who would believe in a character who not only survived the ligaturing of an artery in a gangrenous leg but who fell off a hay wagon in a freshly plowed field and had the heavy wooden wheel of the wagon roll over his head? If the field had not just been plowed, his skull would undoubtedly have been crushed. As it was, he had a bad headache for a few days.

Who would believe that, not long after the move to Florida, Grandfather stood on the beach, looking out over the ocean, with colleagues on either side of him, and remained standing when a bolt of lightning from a sudden tropical storm felled and killed the other two men?

When Grandfather neared middle age, he got Bright's disease. He knew that it was fatal, and that his life expectancy was limited. His eyes suffered the kind of massive deterioration which is the result of badly diseased kidneys. But Grandfather was by no means prepared to die. He had a pitcher of water by his side at all times, and he drank countless glasses of water—Florida sulphur water. Not only did he recover from Bright's disease, but he went down in medical annals as the first person whose eyes had deteriorated from kidney disease who recovered his full vision. I remember him sitting, when he was in his nineties, in the library after dinner reading *The Wall Street Journal.* His red chair is now in the Tower, and perhaps it has brought with it a measure of his courage—and stubbornness.

In his early sixties, when he was living in Scotland, he was told that his heart was in very bad shape and would not last a year. Grandfather's response was to go mountain climbing. He would climb until he fainted. When he came to, he would pick himself up and climb until he fainted again—a rather unorthodox way of curing a heart condition.

He had passage on the *Lusitania* ("But *not* the *Titanic,* too," Mother would say, lest I get carried away) and canceled it at the last minute to have dinner with an old friend.

Who would believe Grandfather?

When he first went South he still had the West in his speech and manners, and he met Caroline

L'Engle, my Dearma, through her two older brothers. She was as immediately attracted to his Western virility as he to her subtle Southern charm. They were married when she was twenty and he was twenty-two.

It was not a happy marriage. Mother said that between the South and the West there was always the barrier of the manner of living, and this must have been exacerbated because the old manner of living in the South had been taken away by the war; all that the old Southerners had left was who they were, and they held on to social amenities, the small and gentle graces. They wore elegant gowns and suits which were completely impractical for the new, impoverished way of life, but which were all they had. Dearma was married in a made-over ball gown of her mother's; the children's clothes were cut out of the salvageable material of their parents' wardrobes.

Social life was topsy-turvy. "Nobody who had money was anybody," said Mother, and the suspicion of "new money" remained with her always. During the day the young men who were most desirable as escorts to the St. Cecilia Ball or the Patriarch Dances might be selling groceries or working in a pharmacy. "A young man in an apron might sell you a slab of bacon, and present himself at your door in rusty dinner clothes in the evening."

Many things worked against my grandparents' marriage from the start. Add to the differences between South and West, and the general poverty and hardship (all the children were undernourished, many of them rickety, and many not strong enough to survive the normal childhood ailments), that both of them were strong-willed and dominant. No wonder there was conflict in Mother's childhood home.

2

MOTHER'S MATERNAL GRANDMOTHER, the Madeleine L'Engle after whom I am named, was probably the strongest influence in her life, and had led a completely different kind of life from the Kansas grandparents'; they might have been from different planets. I know her as Mado, a French nickname for Madeleine; and I think of her generation and my further forebears by the names Mother used. A Southern family is usually impossible to sort out; after the immediate uncles and aunts and first cousins, little distinction is made between second, third, and far more distant cousins; they are kin, and that is all that matters.

For me, my mother's Papa is Grandfather, and her Mama is Dearma; and if Mother told me fewer stories about Dearma than about her grandparents and great-grandparents, it is partly because I knew Dearma for myself. I did not need stories to make her come alive for me. And it may also have been because Mother often fled the tensions at home to stay with Mado, with Amma and Ampa, with favorite cousins, and she preferred to limit her reminiscences to happy ones.

There might not have been so much storytelling

had I not been an only child, and had we not traveled so much. Mother whiled away the time on trains, in hotels in strange cities, in restaurants, by the remembrance of things past. The stories were a foundation of security which helped her, I'm sure, as much as they helped me during the insecurity of our nomadic life. The precariousness of both my parents' health; the uncertainty of Father's ability to pay bills—for his work was not going well; the confusion of living in a world so caught in the grip of a great Depression that only a terrible war could bring a semblance of prosperity: all this must have been far more difficult for my mother than I could begin to guess. Her stories helped us both.

I do not know Mother's physical genetic pattern, who left the strongest imprint on her DNA; but Amma and Ampa, Mado, and Greatie are the ones who left indelible imprints on her psychic genetic pattern.

Mother's name, like mine, came from her maternal great-grandmother, and I learned that Mother spoke most often of Mado when she was depressed, because Mado, even in recollection, brought the gift of laughter. She was born Madeleine Saunders, in Charleston, South Carolina, and when she was a young girl her father was ambassador to the court of Spain. Mado was his hostess, because her mother was in poor health. Countess Eugénie Montijo, later to become the wife of Napoleon III and Empress of France, was Mado's closest friend. They had clothes made to match (Dearma's wedding dress came from the Spanish court days), rode together, hunted together, daydreamed together. It was a life of countless balls and great dinner parties. Some years ago, Mother gave me the huge silver tray on which after-dinner coffee was served in the Embassy; it is heavy to lift with nothing on it, and after-dinner coffee in Spain included not only coffee but a large silver pitcher full of hot milk.

The golden world of those dinner parties is something out of a fairy tale to me. It was a world in which the rules of etiquette were fixed and unmovable. One of the table services was of gold (it's long gone, but I would love to have had a glance at it), and one evening Mado almost disgraced herself when a golden spoon fell to the floor and she started to bend down to pick it up, then caught the formidable eye of her ambassador father. She sat through the rest of the meal in misery while the beautiful spoon was trampled beyond repair, because it was not etiquette for any of the servants to pick it up, or acknowledge that it had fallen.

I think of the frequent entertaining Hugh and I do, both here at Crosswicks and in New York, where I am hostess and cook—he, host and butler; of the casualness of it, the laughter and warmth and good conversation, and I would not change it—even all those dishes to wash later. But, just as I would have liked a glimpse of that golden spoon, so too would I have liked to sit in on one of those court dinners.

The change in ways of living has come slowly, and has increased with each of the wars. One night last winter I came home from a full day's work and started to get ready for a dinner party. Much of the cooking I had done the night before, but there's always a lot to do on the day itself, and I remarked to Hugh, who was helping me, "When Mother gave a dinner party she lay down all the afternoon before, and someone extra was brought in to help so the cook and maid wouldn't get too tired."

Mado herself was aware that the world was not all feasting and fun; as my parents anticipated change and difficulty, so did Mado; one day she and Eugénie and Eugénie's brothers were talking about the necessity for physical courage and endurance, and to prove their own stamina, each took a knife and plunged it into the flesh of the forearm.

I try to visualize these fairy-tale balls, these essays in bravery on the part of the young grandees and Mado. Mother said that her grandmother had a beautiful singing voice and played the guitar, and "charmed the Spanish grandees with her voice," and with her open, childlike friendliness, warmth of manner, and quick pleasure in all beauty.

And I remember,

> *Fear no more the heat o' the sun,*
> *Nor the furious winter's rages;*
> *Thou thy worldly task hast done,*
> *Home art gone, and ta'en thy wages;*
> *Golden lads and girls all must,*
> *As chimney-sweepers, come to dust.*

It was a long time before Mado herself came to dust, for she lived to be a very old lady; but the fairy-tale days of court ended when she returned to the American South. When I look at her pictures, and the only ones I have are of her as an old woman, I am humbled by the serenity and joy in her face, there is never a trace of bitterness or resentment, and she had much cause for both. I see also quiet strength, silent endurance; she had need of the courage for which she and Eugénie and the young grandees tested themselves.

She married a young army surgeon, William

Johnson L'Engle, whose family was from Charleston, but who was living in North Florida. I have a picture of him which always gives me a poignant stab; it was taken shortly before his untimely death, and this strong, slightly arrogant young man looks so much like Bion that his school friends have remarked, "Hey, Bion, that's a great picture. When did you have it taken?" And yet Bion looks like Hugh, and I find this genetic paradox delightful.

When William L'Engle was commissioned, he wrote that his successful examination has "relieved my mind of a load of anxiety . . . and I have the certainty of a comfortable income as long as I live. I will write you again when I reach Charleston and let you know when to expect me. . . ."

The army commission made William free to marry Mado, and it was a new freedom for him, because his parents were living as pioneer a life in Florida as Amma and Ampa in Kansas. When William was eleven he wrote to his Aunt Leonis L'Engle Johnson, in Charleston, "Father has failed entirely this year; he has made no corn and the caterpillars have made a clear sweep of all his cotton, and everybody else shares the same fate." I am awed at the education which these unschooled children received at home. In the same letter eleven-year-old William writes of his brothers and sisters, "Edward is nine. He will soon be able to write you. Mary is almost six, and is improving fast. She reads well, and sews well; she has just commenced writing and little Johnnie, too, begins to spell. He has just recovered from a fit of ague. My health is feeble, but no fever. . . . Remember me to all my Charleston friends. . . ." Another time, not long after, he wrote, "Father is engaged near Hibernia, cutting timber. As usual, it is a hard life and not a very profitable one."

The cousin to whom William wrote most often was Miller Hallowes, whose plantation was called Bolingbroke—what lovely, otherworldly names the family houses had: Bolingbroke, Palermo, Hibernia, the names of the Old World translated to the new. Miller Hallowes (who was almost a father to William) had, when he was nineteen years old, left his native England and gone to South America to offer his services to Bolivar. Young Hallowes and Bolivar became close friends, and the Englishman "fought in the wars of Independence for eleven years continuously," and at Bolivar's death he was given the last portrait ever painted of the great hero, as a token of friendship and esteem.

He had gone home to England, and came to America only to see to some property his mother had inherited. He expected to stay in America for a few weeks, but he fell in love and married and stayed until his death in 1877. I would guess that the flora and fauna of the Southern territory reminded him of Venezuela, and that he had become accustomed to a warmer climate than England's.

He was a good friend to William, and later to Mado, and Bolingbroke was always open to them.

William, graduating from medical school before he was twenty-one, was ambitious, probably because of the hard conditions of his childhood, but his ambition was more for his family than for himself and he must have had the gift of healing in his hands and heart, for the medical methods of the day, as he describes them in his letters, make one wonder how anyone survived the prescribed treatments.

Mado and William were married on April 3, 1854, and there was a yellow-fever epidemic in Key West in June. William, who was considered an authority on epidemics, was sent for and left, evidently in a rush, for he forgot his glass retorts at Bolingbroke. Mado followed him as soon as she could arrange for his medical supplies and her guitar to be sent by ship from Savannah to Key West.

In the autumn of 1856 William was sent by the U.S. Army to the Department of the Pacific. Many years later, his daughter, my Dearma, wrote, "They crossed the Isthmus of Darien, now the Panama Canal. My father wanted to give my mother some pear-shaped pearls, but my mother declined the gift on account of the expense of the journey—their baggage alone cost fifty dollars to transport over the railroad. He bought her instead a little china basket of fruit, which she treasured always. It was saved from the great fire in 1901." This was the appalling fire which burned the entire city of Jacksonville, and I shall get to it in its proper chronology.

It was while they were stationed out West that their first child, a son, was born. Mado, with the *joie de vivre* which I have come to think of as her dominant trait, was not held down by motherhood. She went with the other officers' wives from post to post, in rough wooden wagons, to dances. The baby was rolled in a shawl and put on a bed among all the wraps, and she would go in and nurse him whenever he was hungry, and then go on dancing till sunrise. She was adaptable, my great-grandmother. These dances at rough army posts must have been very different from the balls at the Spanish court, or the St. Cecilia Ball in Charleston, and yet I doubt very much if she made comparisons. She seems to have had the ability to stand firmly on the rock of her past while living completely and unregretfully in the present. My mother's adaptability came to her both by blood and by example.

Mado's second child was born while she was on a vacation with her parents, and the third, my grandmother, Dearma, in an adobe hut in Camp Mason, Texas.

When it became apparent that a war between the states was inevitable, William resigned his commission in the United States Army and applied for one in the Confederate Army. As far as I can gather, both William and Mado felt that the cause of the South was a just one, and that the real issues had little to do with slavery. It is impossible to understand their feelings from hindsight; we know too much; and we see things from a perspective impossible to them. But Mado never lost her joy, despite all the tragedy which was to come to her, and this may be what makes me know that she and William were never dishonorable or dishonest in their thinking or in their behavior.

3

AT THE BEGINNING of the war William was called to the house of Senator Mallory in Lake City, Florida, why, I do not know, because the senator and his wife were not at home. William was having a bout of the malaria which almost everybody endured in chronic form, and sent to the pharmacy for quinine, which, in those days, was put up as a powder. A mistake was made—on purpose? by accident? no one ever knew—and he was sent morphine instead of quinine, and took a large dose. He realized quickly what had happened, and called the servants and told them to walk him up and down, make him drink hot coffee, and under no conditions to let him go to sleep. All the time that they were walking him, giving him coffee, the servants said that he kept groaning, "My God, my wife and children! My God, my wife and children!"

By morning the servants were exhausted, and he thought that the danger was over and told them to go to bed and get some rest. And then he died.

Remember William, dying alone,
Buried under an alien stone.

The flesche is brukle, the Fiend is sle;
Timor mortis conturbat me.

The confusion of war swept over his death; it was not until his sons were grown that they were able to find out where he was buried.

Mado was left penniless at the beginning of the war, with three small children, and everything else taken away from her. For a while she was matron of a military hospital at Lake City, Florida, and, typically, nursed Northern and Southern soldiers with equal tenderness, for in her heart there was no North nor South. "Many Northern boys died in her arms," Mother told me. "One mother and father of a Yankee soldier were so grateful for her care of their son that they sent her a ring with a beautiful black pearl. It burned up in the great fire with so many other of our treasures."

Illness and death were daily companions in her life. She never ceased to grieve for her husband, but it was a quiet, personal grief; what she offered others was loving care and laughter. She wore only black and white for the rest of her life, though she did not carry an aura of mourning with her, but one of complete zest for life. She could have married many times over, but William the golden lad was the love of her life, and when she lay dying at the age of eighty-seven, she kept calling his name. She also asked for a dish of ice cream, which she ate with great appreciation and pleasure, and died shortly thereafter. Living or dying, I don't think Mado feared the heat of the sun.

Just after William's death, Mado wrote a long letter to her cousin Caro Hallowes at Bolingbroke, offering her services in nursing eighteen-year-old Katie Hallowes, who was desperately ill. Despite her own grief, she was able to feel intense compassion for Caro's young daughter. And she added, "How often I have wished since Katie's illness that my precious husband could have been spared, if only for a little while longer, to be with you in this trial. He stood so high as a physician and was such a good, patient nurse."

Letters were long in those days, partly because there was no such thing as instant communication. Mado says, "I did not write to you last week as I was anxiously expecting a letter from you to tell us of Katie's welfare. You know how deeply I sympathize with you, dear Cousin, in your distress and anxiety, and I long for tomorrow's mail hoping that it may bring me a letter to say that Katie is better. We cannot get any letters which may come by the St. Johns [river] until Sunday afternoon, and as the steamer for Savannah returns early Monday morning and Father does not often send to town, we have no means of answering our letters by return mail."

She ends this particular letter, written from Palermo on July 6, 1861: "My paper and time are limited. I would not under any other circumstances ask you, dear Cousin, but do you remember the conversation I had with you in regard to the likeness of William which you have? that it was taken by William for me, and in case of anything happening to him was to belong to me. You will not blame me, I am sure, for claiming it now. I want you please to send it to me here, and I will have a copy of it taken for you, which I will send to you."

I'm grateful that Mother has given me copies of some of Mado's letters which have survived, for they show me glimpses of her ability to accept change, and surely her world changed even more radically than our own. Her friendships were forever; she had continued her friendship with Eugénie when the princess became Empress of France. They wrote long letters, which perished in the great fire. She seems to have been surrounded constantly by children, her own, and various nephews, nieces, and cousins. Only once is there a deep figurative sigh as she remarks on the bliss of a day alone.

During the difficult years between 1861 and 1865 Mado remained in Florida. It was so hot in summer that it was difficult to sleep; one of the little boys remarked, "Oh, Mama, my head is as wet as a bowl of water." It was cold in winter, but they were able to keep tolerably warm because of plentiful fat pine wood.

She wrote another cousin and friend: "This farm is like most farms, surrounded outside the yard by cultivated lands with the usual feature in Southern landscapes, dry girdled pines, and would look dreary if there were not a fringe of date palm trees. Near here, about a quarter of a mile or more, but the path leading to it passing the cultivated fields, there is a beautiful little lake surrounded by high banks densely covered with tall magnolia, cypress, hickory, and live oak trees.

"It is too hot a journey to undertake very often as we must return right in the heat of the day, if we stay. Yesterday we took our work and a very pleasant book, *In and Around Stamboul,* by Mrs. Hornby, and Henry read aloud to us, whilst we sat on the bank under the shade of a large magnolia, and sewed, and watched a dozen wild ducks in pairs, chattering and diving for fish in the lake, and every now and then skimming over the surface. Occasionally a large, white crane goes sailing by, much to Lena's [Dearma's] delight, who with the other children are gathered around Minerva at a short distance, watching her string the red berries of a species of running box, which I think quite pretty.

"It is so dark I cannot see the letters I form. I have written this last page in darkness, but now have lit my candle to continue. We do not use many candles here as tallow is scarce and one dollar or more a pound, but instead have brilliant fires of the fattest kind of lightwood. I do not hesitate to read by it as it really gives such a bright light, though I would never attempt to sew. I generally knit or read after tea for an hour or so. A candle is lit during supper and afterwards blown out."

It would be difficult to guess from her letters how near actual starvation the family often came; how much energy was expended on nursing the ill; and how equal love and energy had at all times to be available for Dearma and her brothers; how many hours were spent in transforming old brocade curtains or silk bedspreads into clothes for the children. Some of Dearma's dresses and the boys' suits were made of the beautiful velvets and satins of Mado's gowns from the Spanish court, completely inappropriate for their Spartan way of life, and an ironic comment.

If she cried alone at night she does not say. What she shared was love and laughter, and I am grateful for her.

4

At the close of the War between the States, Mado managed to get back to her parents, who were then living in Raleigh, North Carolina, "where they were quietly starving to death," Mother wrote me once, "because they had lost everything during the war."

And here is a perfect example of the extraordinary interdependence of all things. Years before, while William and Mado were out in Washington Territory with the United States Army, they became close friends of General Custer, through whom they acquired an Irish cook, the wife of one of his soldiers. During the war this soldier became an officer, "and by one of those strange streaks of fortune, became Captain of the Garrison in Raleigh, N.C." One day a United States commissary wagon drove up, and on the seat beside the driver was the captain's lady, Mado's ex-cook. The two women embraced; the cook took one horrified look at Mado and her family, and brought them desperately needed food. Mother added, "When finally some of the ladies of the town brought themselves to call on the Captain's wife, she put on an apron and, answering the doorbell herself, said the lady was not at home."

It makes me wonder what harvest my own most casual actions may reap; surely Mado never thought that her instinctive loving courtesy to all people would one day be a matter of life and death. Her little daughter, my grandmother, might well have died without the food the captain's lady brought, and I would not be here to write about any of this today.

Mado died a year before I was born, and yet I feel that I have always known her, the stories about her are so vivid. I have never heard her name mentioned by anybody in our enormous Southern clan without its evoking a smile. There have been several Montague-Capulet schisms in my mother's family, but I have never heard an unloving word about Mado.

In a day when grandchildren were supposed to revere and be formal with their grandparents, her many grandchildren adored her, and no one remembers being scolded by her. One of my favorite cousins reports that the closest her grandmother ever came to reproving her was once when Tracy referred to President Theodore Roosevelt as "Teddy." Mado said, "My child, I wish to hear you call him Mr. Roosevelt. He may be a Republican, but, after all, he is the President of the United States."

Another time while Tracy was a student at Wellesley and was home for vacation, her grandmother slipped into French, as naturally as though she were speaking English, and Tracy could not understand, and stopped her. She said that Mado "only smiled gently, and with a little twinkle in her eye replied, 'I beg your pardon, since you are going to college I thought you were being educated.' "

Perhaps the fact that I write at all is a result of

Mado's passion for education. She did not think the schooling in North Carolina or Florida adequate for her children; I don't know why she did not go home to Charleston, but went instead to Winchester, Virginia. Possibly she could not afford Charleston, but could eke out a living in Winchester by taking in boarders, or ill people, and nursing them. The boys went through college, and Dearma to the Virginia Episcopal Institute for Young Ladies—how pompous that sounds, but the girls there were given an education which isn't even available to girls today, Episcopal, ladies, or no. Mado herself had been well taught, and was willing to go hungry, to work long hours, stay up with a patient all night, in order to give her children the learning she treasured. And I'm sure she herself taught her children far more than she realized. I know that not only has my mother taught me many things I never learned in school, but also that the summer Josephine turned three, Mother spent patient hours playing with her, and by the end of the summer Jo could read and write the alphabet and spell out simple words, and the whole process was a game for her.

I wonder what I will be able to teach my grandchildren? Not much, this summer, except for a few folk songs and nursery rhymes when I sing them to sleep.

Did Mado ever have the sudden, intemperate rages which sometimes hit me, and which are produced by what seems completely inadequate cause?

She surely had reason for rage and resentment, and yet these are qualities which are never mentioned in regard to her. If they were there, she kept them to herself, and healed them in her own way, with prayer. I have her battered Bible, which Mother had rebound for me. It was much read, much marked, and there are stains which came, I think, through private tears. Perhaps through it she will teach me an alphabet of grace. She had that spontaneous quality of aliveness which illuminates people who have already done a lot of their dying, and I think I am beginning to understand the truth of that.

"My grandmother," Mother said of Mado, "was an incurable romantic, reading and rereading her favorite romantic stories and poems until her death." And yet no one could accuse Mado of having had a protected life, or of losing her grip on reality.

I need my own equivalent of the picaresque novels which may have reminded Mado of the lost years of the Spanish court—although it never occurred to her to bemoan them or try to return to them. I have occasional binges of reading English murder mysteries or science fiction, not so much as an escape but as a reminder that there is still honor and fidelity in the world, despite murder and crime; and that the sky above me is full of billions of solar systems and island galaxies, and that nobody has yet been able to put the creation of a galaxy into the language of provable fact.

We are a generation out of touch with reality. The "realistic" novels push me further away from the truth of things, rather than bringing me closer. We cannot make mystery and miracle acceptable by trying to constrict them into the language of the laboratory or the television commercial.

All that, in finite terms, is left of Mado is her

Bible, some yellowed letters, a few pieces of once beautiful furniture, its veneer buckling from age and exposure to salt air. But there is more to her than that, and it is the mystery of her *ousia* which helps me to see a little more clearly through the dimness of human understanding.

I do not want to romanticize about Mother's senility. I know that there is no turning back the clogging of the arteries, and that there is nothing to look forward to but further decline. But if I stop here I am blocked in my loving, just as her thinking is blocked by atherosclerosis.

I try to accept the bare factual truth of Mother's condition, as Mado accepted loss and death; and yet I remember Tallis saying once that "we are not interested in the love of truth *as against* the truth of love." This does not mean that we are not interested in the love of truth; his statement is one which I have to try to understand with all of me, not just my conscious mind. The love of truth without the truth of love is usually cold and cruel, I have found. The truth of love can sometimes be irrational, absurd, and yet it is what makes us grow toward maturity, opens us to joy. Mado, holding a dying Yankee soldier in her arms, was witness to the irrationality of the truth of love. This kind of truth is often painful; it must have been so for her, and I am certainly finding it true in this household this summer. But it is all that gets me through each day.

5

"TELL ME A STORY, MOTHER . . ."

"Well, tell me a story about when Greatie was a little girl."

Greatie: my mother's great-grandmother; William L'Engle's mother; Mado's mother-in-law; Susan Philippa Fatio.

How much will Léna and Charlotte remember of their great-grandmother? They have never known my mother as a full human being, but only as an ancient old woman with the strange title of the Great-grandmother, which they cannot yet pronounce, and so they will remember her mostly through the stories their mother and I tell them when they, too, say, "Tell me a story . . . Tell me a story about Gracchi."

Josephine and Maria and Bion have living memories of their great-grandfather; Jo was eleven when he died. I didn't know any of my greats, but I feel close to Greatie because Mother has given her to me.

Greatie and her parents were as much pioneers as Amma and Ampa and yet, in the early days of North Florida settling, there was an aura of cosmopolitanism and courtliness completely missing in the West. Greatie spoke French, Italian, Spanish, German; read Latin and Greek. She had a vast store of folk and fairy tales from all lands which she told and retold her children, grandchildren, and great-grandchildren. "The one I remember best," Mother said, "is the Spanish folk tale of Don Rat Humperez and Cockroachie Martínez."

The Fatios were originally from Sicily, and left home because of political upheaval and religious persecution; some settled in Italy, some in France, Spain, Switzerland. Why Greatie's father, François Philippe Fatio, came from Switzerland to the New World, and to North Florida in particular, I do not know.

Mother's personal memories of Greatie are, of course, of a very old lady living in quiet poverty; but these last years of Susan Philippa Fatio's life, austere though they were, must have seemed strangely uneventful to the old lady. How many homes were burned out from under her? I'm not sure; I've counted up to six.

"Once upon a time when Greatie was a little girl," Mother said, during that winter of inner and outer cold in Chamonix, while we sat huddled in sweaters and drank countless cups of tea to keep warm, "she was living with her parents on their plantation called New Switzerland on the St. Johns River." One day one of the servants came rushing to them through the woods in great excitement and told them that the Indians were preparing to attack and were going to scalp the entire family. François Philippe refused to believe them, because the Indians had always been friendly with the family. But New Switzerland was caught in the middle of a war between the Indians and Andrew Jackson's forces; the Indians had been unfairly attacked, and they were so angry that they were out to scalp all whites in their path, even those who had been their friends. Two faithful servants, Dublin and Scipio, held François Philippe bodily to keep him from going to reason with the Indians, persuaded him that they were beyond reason at that moment, and urged the entire household into a boat which was always kept at the dock. Scipio had been polishing the table knives and carried them into the boat, "and so the knives were the only possession saved from the fire. Greatie told us that shots followed them across the river and splashed into the water, and why nobody was hit she never knew . . ."

Their next home was burned, too, by vindictive arsonists. Greatie and her family were constantly being caught in the middle of someone else's fight. There was the battle for the Floridas, as the large, southernmost territory was then known; the Fatios lived in a section which passed back and forth between the Spanish and the English on paper—which didn't affect them nearly as much as border warfare between the Florida settlers and a group of bandits, called "filibusters" by Greatie, who came in from Georgia. One of the filibusters called himself Dictator of the Republic of Florida, and François Philippe fought with the Spaniards against this premature Hitler.

"Shortly after this battle, in which he was nearly killed," Mother said, "the roof of their house in St. Augustine blew off in a storm; it was taken up bodily by the wind and settled on top of the family as they were trying to escape. Can you imagine rushing out of the house and then being trapped under your own roof?"

"What happened?" Of course I knew, but I was breathless with excitement no matter how many times I heard the story.

"They were rescued by Commodore Campbell of the United States Navy, who came to their assistance with his sailors. The family were all bruised and bleeding, but they were lucky to get away without being drowned, because the tide was rising and the streets were soon flooded."

"Did they lose everything again, everything?"

"Everything. This time they didn't even save the knives."

Everything. Nor was this the last time.

And yet Greatie wrote, after they finally rebuilt their home on the St. Johns River, a home of pine logs and cypress bark: "We were well content to be there once more, leading a life of tranquility and ease. My father, when well-supplied with reading matter and the society of a few friends, seemed never dull or dissatisfied. Chess, cards, and backgammon varied the monotony of the repose of country life; and to look out on the river, flowing majestically by, seemed always to charm him. He was sixty-five years of age when we returned to New Switzerland, but full of vigor of mind and body. He was possessed of a cheerful and vivacious disposition, and was witty and full of anecdote. I never tired of listening to his descriptions of Switzerland. I remember one afternoon, when sitting on the piazza with him, his calling my attention to some grandly beautiful clouds looming up on the horizon, across the river, and saying, 'Look, look, my child, before it changes; you cannot have a more perfect picture of Mont Blanc than that cloud gives you; no painter could represent it as well. Call your mother to see it. O beautiful, beautiful!' and his handsome face beamed with pleasure as he gazed at it."

But a life of "tranquility and ease" never seemed to last long for Greatie. "In the year 1836 the homestead at New Switzerland was again destroyed, being burnt by Seminole Indians . . ."

Six years earlier Greatie had married Lieutenant John L'Engle, "of the 3d U.S. Artillery, a graduate of the Military Academy of West Point." She does not say a great deal about him. I would gather that he was a literate and charming man, but also a dreamer and impractical. After her marriage she continues to speak of New Switzerland as home, and so this final burning affected her deeply. She writes, "My father and brother having died within six months of each other, Colonel Miller Hallowes, fourth son of my Aunt Louisa, came from England to receive her share of my grandfather's property, which my father had been taking care of for her." Miller Hallowes was at New Switzerland when the Indians attacked, and he was wounded by a bullet. Scipio, the same Scipio who had helped in the escape at the time of the first New Switzerland fire, helped him into a boat. The Indians went into the house, "feasted and drank, dancing and yelling, cut up the piano, and finally set fire to and destroyed the houses with their contents. The houses have never been rebuilt."

Greatie, the teller and writer of tales, was wistful that "in all our wanderings there were no schools or other educational opportunities" for the younger Fatio children. Five of the children received formal schooling, but "Leonora and I had no such advantages. Fortunately for us we both loved books and, more fortunately still, our parents were educated persons, lovers of learning and culture, who took pleasure in imparting knowledge to us. To them we were indebted for all we learned."

No wonder her son, William, was able to write letters to Cousin Miller Hallowes and Aunt Leonis when he was only eleven years old.

Greatie had also memorized reams, and could recite, with flourish and pleasure, from her favorite books, ranging from Plato and the Bible to romantic novelists. This huge store of memory stood her in good stead, for she was blind during her last years. But she lost none of her storytelling ability, or her complete recall of all that she had learned.

"Tell me about Greatie and the African princess."

That was probably my favorite story about Greatie. A wealthy planter and slave trader fell in love with an African princess, and married her. She lived in his huge house partly as wife, partly as servant, bore him many children, and nearly died of homesickness. She was ostracized by both whites and blacks, except for Greatie, who once a week was rowed down the river—it must have been a two- or three-hour trip in the grizzling sun—to spend the day with the princess. First Greatie had to have lunch with the slave trader, while the princess served them. Then Greatie and the princess went off together to the princess's rooms, and talked, and drank cold tea together.

If Mado had strong ideas about what was right and what was wrong in human relationships, so did her mother-in-law. Greatie and the princess were close friends in a day when such a friendship was unheard of, and Greatie simply laughed when she was criticized and sometimes slandered because of this relationship. I was delighted when I learned, only recently, that a good friend of mine is a descendant of this long-gone African princess.

"Tell me the story about Greatie and the pirate."

In the old days of our country when there were many small clusters of settlers in tiny villages which are now large cities, it was the custom for the people in the "big house" to take in travelers for the night, or longer.

One winter a charming Frenchman, Monsieur Dupont, came through the township of San Pablo, in which the young Greatie was living. He was grateful for hospitality for "a night or two," and spent the winter. He was a witty conversationalist; his manners were courteously impeccable; he was a fine musician and he and Greatie played duets by the hour. When at last he left, with many declarations of affection all round, he gave her some of his music and books; and it was only when leafing through them that she saw his signature and discovered the real identity of her guest: Jean Laffite, the famous pirate.

6

THEY ARE ALL DEAD, long dead, these golden lads and lasses, so long dead that the taint of corruption no longer clings to their dust. They are all gone, François Philippe, Dublin and Scipio, the African princess and the French pirate. Greatie is remembered only by a few remaining great-grandchildren.

And by me.

> *The flesche is brukle, the Fiend is sle;*
> Timor mortis conturbat me.

Mother said once, "What a passion for education my forebears had!" When I think that Greatie was never formally schooled, it makes me wonder about the present-day school system. These "uneducated" women, Greatie, Mado, my mother, were fluent in more languages, had a far greater background in classics and world history, than most college graduates today.

There was a tradition in the L'Engle family, the Fatio family, that every child in the household should be taught to read and write at an early age, and the children of the servants learned their letters side by side with the children of the family. Interesting; in every single family letter I have come across, the Negroes are always referred to as servants, never as slaves; and service, at that time, had not taken on the connotation of drudgery it now has; it was an honorable word; and if the Negroes on the plantations served their L'Engle and Fatio masters, the masters likewise served their servants.

Maybe there were Simon Legrees in my family but they made little impression on my mother. And I do not believe that she has given me an overidealized picture of Greatie or of Mado; they are very alive for me, rounded, full, erudite women with all kinds of human flaws (which have come down to me): quick tempers, impetuousness, opinionatedness. But they are real. I respect them and love them. I try not to let them down, but I know that when I do, they would understand and expect me to pick myself up, shake off the dust, and start right over.

I'm grateful that Mado and Greatie are part of my roots. I'm unusually fortunate in Mother's repertoire of stories, as wide as Greatie's. My Oklahoman husband knows little of his roots, which is a loss.

Pride of family: is there a difference between pride of family and respect for a family tradition and responsibility to it? I think so, although I have seen people whose pride in ancestry is sheer snobbery and seems to provide only an excuse for laziness and ungenerosity of spirit.

Mado had the most generous of hearts; if I am mean of heart I am letting her down, as well as myself. Greatie had compassion and true friendship for a black woman at a time when such a thing was unheard of. Dearma visited those in jail and fought for prison reform long before it became a *cause célèbre*.

The first hospital in the Deep South with beds for blacks came into being because of the vision of one of Mado's grandsons. These are very small drops in the bucket, but they came at times when the bucket was nearly empty, and they give me a tradition of compassion and generosity to live up to. This is Mother's family, because this is Mother's book, but there are examples of courage and nobility in Father's family, too. And, on both sides, there are examples of meanness and selfishness and greed. A vast, closely knit family such as Mother's had its full share of scandals and skeletons in the closet. Most of these I did not learn from her, and since they were sometimes told me with intent to hurt, they have little place in this book.

If I continue my journey through the past, beyond Mother, Dearma, Mado, Greatie, I come to forebears who settled in Charleston, South Carolina, well before the American Revolution. They were a conglomeration of French Huguenots fleeing religious persecution, and Frenchmen who had come to Ireland at the time of the Norman conquest, who had been given huge grants of land, and later had to flee Ireland when these same grants were taken away from them by Henry VIII's Cromwell, a kind of rude justice.

The name, the unpronounceable name of L'Engle, was originally de l'Angle, which is considerably easier. One spring when we were driving through château country, Mother told me that Dearma had gone looking for the de l'Angle château, and found it. Dearma stood outside the rusty wrought-iron gates and looked across the overgrown gardens to the château. An old woman in black was cutting roses, and hobbled up to the gates to ask Dearma if she could help her. "Mama told her who she was and why she had come, and the old woman said, 'Oh, you're one of the American cousins,' and asked her in to tea."

"But how did the name get from de l'Angle to L'Engle?"

"The story goes that during the rough years of the Reformation, two de l'Angle brothers quarreled over their religious convictions. The French Huguenot brother not only fled France to save his life, he was so angry with his brother that he changed his name." L'Engle: my Southern kin pronounce it Langul; my Northern kin pronounce it Longle. I find it simplest to say it the way it looks: Lengel.

I asked Mother, "When he changed his name, where did he go?"

"He fled with his family to Santo Domingo, and became a planter. But the pattern of building a home and a way of life and then having to leave everything and flee is constant in our family. There was a bloody and violent uprising, and once again he had to take his wife and children and flee for his life. He set sail for the United States, and outside Charleston his ship was caught in a violent storm and wrecked. Only two lives were saved, two of the L'Engle children, a boy and a girl."

The two orphans were taken into the household of Judge William Johnson, and brought up with his children. Both, I think, married Johnsons, but here my genealogy is confused. Greatie's husband, John L'Engle, was an adopted son of William Johnson's. Mado is the one who is a direct descendant of the old judge; he was her grandfather; her mother was Anna Hayes Johnson; so she and William were cousins, but not by blood. Mother knew how it all worked out, and I should have written it down long ago, but somehow it never occurred to me that there might be a time like this, when she cannot tell me.

I'm proud of that distant ancestor, William Johnson; he was Jefferson's first appointee to the Supreme Court, the youngest justice to sit on the bench, and the first dissenting justice. Like most of my family, he was opinionated, articulate, and cared passionately about justice. While I was writing a novel set in the Deep South, *The Other Side of the Sun,* I had to do a good bit of research; my English school taught me more about the Wars of the Roses than about the American Revolution. I was delighted to come across William Johnson's name as a man who stood up for the rights of the black man, both slave and free.

After a slave uprising in Charleston, many restrictions were put on all Negroes, and a law was passed that no slave might be taught to read or write. Judge Johnson was infuriated at this gross injustice, and announced to the Supreme Court that he considered it unconstitutional.

It is a present responsibility to be his descendant. He has left his mark on my genetic pattern, whether I like it or not. Because he came to me, not as a personage out of history, but as a living character in Mother's stories, he has also left his mark on my memory, and so has given me the strength on occasion to speak out and take unpopular stands.

Mother's most treasured possession is a huge portrait of Judge Johnson's grandchildren, my great-great-grandmother and my great-great-great-aunt, one playing the flute, the other the harp; the harp was one of the losses of the war. The portrait was painted by S. F. B. Morse, the man who invented

Morse code but who was first known as a portrait painter. The two young women it portrays are part of me, as are the old judge, Greatie, Mado. Without them I would be someone else; I would not be me. My forebears have bequeathed to me the basic structure of my own particular pattern, both in my cells and in the underwater areas of my imagination.

I look at Mother huddled in her chair by the window and think once more about Mado and Greatie. In a day of what we would consider primitive medical knowledge, and no nursing or convalescent homes, no hospitals as we understand hospitals today, they both lived to a ripe old age, with their wits about them. Up until Grandfather, there is no record of senility in the family, although there were a few "holy fools," like the twins, Willy and Harry, in *The Other Side of the Sun*.

Obviously, nursing homes have not caused senility in the elderly; but when grandmother or great-grandmother continued to live with the larger family, to be given meaning because she could at least stir the soup or rock the baby, the climate for growing old and dying was more healthy than it is today. I cannot reproduce that climate for Mother. Surgery kept her alive at eighty-seven; antibiotics pulled her through pneumonia at eighty-eight.

For what? For this?

But we cannot turn our backs on scientific progress. I did not want her operated on at eighty-seven until Pat assured me that the tumor in the caecum would cause her great discomfort unless it was removed. I could not tell the doctor not to give her antibiotics for pneumonia.

All I can do is to try not to isolate her; is to hold her when she is afraid; is to accept her as she is, as part of this family, without whom we would be less complete.

7

THE PORTRAITS in my mother's family did not lead a static life, and it is a wonder that as many of them survived as did. During the war, when the Northern conquering troops took over and burned some of my forebears' homes, the portraits—when there was time—were taken away and hidden, and some were never found again.

Mother has hanging in her front hall a not very distinguished oil painting which has always fascinated me, because on the back is painted a crude chess or checkers board, which was used by the occupying soldiers. Many portraits and other paintings were wantonly slashed by sword or knife.

So the family portraits mean a great deal to me, not as an aid to ancestor worship, but as beacons to guide me. I have many more portraits from Mother's family than from Father's, largely because Mother was the eldest of four, and the only girl, and Father was the youngest of ten, and the only surviving male. I have a pastel drawing of Mado as an old woman, done by one of her grandsons, my Uncle Bion. Her face is gentle and tolerant and wise, but I know that behind the compassion in the eyes there is judgment; she did not tolerate dishonor or despair.

My mother learned much from her. I will try to learn, too.

Tell me a story. My granddaughters are already starting the familiar refrain: "Tell a story about when Gracchi was little."

Gracchi's world is gone, as far gone as is my present mother from her *ousia.* As with all worlds, it was good, and it was evil. It had vision, and it was blind. It was rich, and incredibly poor. How can I tell my granddaughters about a world of which I have had no firsthand experience?

If it is impossible for me, it is doubly difficult for my children and trebly for my grandchildren to conceive of a United States in which the entire population was less than that of three of our major cities today.

Jacksonville, now a major city, is bursting at its seams; yet when Mother was a little girl, it was a small town where everybody knew each other, and almost everybody was kin. Family towns are something few people today have known. We're used to living among strangers and near-strangers, with the biological family dispersed north, south, east, west. But when Mother was a little girl, she could walk across the street to Mado's house; it was only a few blocks to Amma and Ampa's.

Shortly after Hugh and I were married we visited Mother, and when she took us to church with her it was definitely not only to go to church, but also to be looked over, and Hugh was appalled that more than half the congregation was kin. Not so today.

Jacksonville, Mother said, was never a typical Southern town. Even before the war, many Northern families had come to Florida, most of them in search of health, but there was little mingling between North and South. After the war, the chasm was even greater.

Mother was born in Amma and Ampa's house, just a year after her parents' marriage. There was at that time no such thing as a hospital or a trained nurse in Jacksonville, and when Dearma became very ill shortly after Mother's birth, nursing her was not easy. In those days it was thought unhealthy to have kitchen or bathroom in the house; the kitchen was a separate building behind the house. Mado and friends and relatives did the nursing, and there were plenty of relatives.

William L'Engle had been the second of twelve children, all educated by Greatie, and Mother's childhood was spent near a great number of aunts and uncles and cousins. Because of the vast age spans, generations were mixed up—one twelve-year-old boy bragged about dandling his great-uncle on his knee.

Mother wrote, "When I was a little girl, I loved Louisa May Alcott's books: *Little Women, Little Men, Eight Cousins.* As I look back now I can see the similarity in my life and *Eight Cousins.*" There were always plenty of children to play with, aunts and uncles to run to for comfort. Life more or less revolved around St. John's Church, and at the four corners of the church lived four great-uncles and their large, multigeneration families.

Play was simple. The girls had large collections of paper dolls, with enormous wardrobes which they painted by hand, and swapped around. For money they used bent pins. Because life at home was often tense and oppressive, Mother spent a great deal of time playing in the homes of varied cousins. She wrote, "The Daniel family life centered around the big student lamp on the dining table. There the family congregated in the evenings, reading aloud, playing games, studying lessons. I spent many happy hours in that magic circle. It was a warm, loving, family life. Tiny Aunt Emmy, with her little black shawl around her shoulders, her hair parted in the middle and coiled in a big knot at the back of her head, could still play the guitar and sing the old songs of the War between the States and the period before.

"Cold winter nights we cousins used to roast potatoes in a little brick oven out in the yard. No potatoes have ever tasted so good. In the evening after our early suppers, we played hare and hounds. The hare had a bag filled with tiny pieces of paper. After a good head start, the hare began to drop the pieces of paper, with the hounds behind him in hot pursuit, following the scent."

There were many picnics on the banks of the St. Johns River. The great river which François Philippe had so loved is tidal, and salty, and, said Mother, is "the only navigable river that flows in the same direction as the Nile." The trees near their favorite picnic place had enormous wild grapevines hanging on them which made wonderful swings.

Sometimes the cousins, sitting on the floor of a big dray pulled by a mule, would be driven out near Palermo to a sugar-cane plantation, for the sugar-boiling. "I can remember how the hot thick syrup would burn our fingers when we pulled the taffy. We usually pulled in couples. It was hard to get started with our great wad of red-hot syrup, but once we got it going, it was great fun to watch the candy in the making. We would get farther and farther away from each other, while the candy got whiter all the time. The experts could braid it, but we children were usually content with a long rope."

Another activity which qualified as play for the children was taking flowers to the cemetery. In those days of large families and high mortality, my mother and her cousins were well acquainted with death. A scarlet-fever epidemic wiped out four first cousins in one week; malaria weakened resistance; yellow fever was a constant threat. The children who had survived whooping cough and measles and the various lethal fevers went regularly to the cemetery with lilies and amaryllis and cape jessamine, and decorated the graves. "So," Mother said, "I have never had any fear of cemeteries but find them a peaceful place."

When the children were a little older most of them had learned to play the piano or the guitar, the flute or the harp, and sang, and one of their games (which Mother and I used to play, too) was tapping out the rhythm of a song or the theme of a symphony, and seeing who could guess first what the melody was.

Mother's Papa had a fine library, through which she was free to browse, and he was also a superb storyteller to his children. By the time I came along, he had lost the ability or the desire to tell stories. But when Mother and her brothers were little, he told imaginative and fantastic tales every night, in front of the fire on chilly winter evenings, sitting on the steps at the foot of the ramp to the beach in summer. Mother, and later on, her brothers, would sit by him, leaning against his knee and keeping one eye on his cigar, because the stories lasted only as long as the cigar lasted.

8

SHE THOUGHT of herself as uneducated and almost illiterate, my mother, because delicate health kept her from completing school. When she was feeling unwell she spent days at a time at Ampa's, curled up in a big leather chair in his library, where there was a set of historical novels by Miss Mulbach—*Empress Josephine, Queen Hortense;* and by Charlotte M. Yonge, *The Dove in the Eagle's Nest* (one of my childhood favorites), *The Heir of Redclyffe;* and she devoured these and many other historical novels ravenously. Ampa also had bound sets of *Harper's* and *Scribner's,* in which *Henry Esmond* and *The Virginian* had come out in monthly installments. With her cousins she read aloud by the hour, around a table in the winter, under the trees by the river bank in the warm weather. This habit of reading aloud, or being read to, remained with Mother all her life. Not only did she read to me when I was little, but she and Father read to each other every night of their lives, Dumas, Dickens, Dostoevsky. This is the first summer she has not enjoyed having our friend Gillian read to her in her clear and pleasant English voice.

Does Mother remember, somewhere deep inside her, any of these years of treasure? She is far better read than I am, the great-grandmother who thinks of herself as being ignorant.

And an ugly duckling who never turned into a swan. Dearma was considered a beauty, and Mother far too often heard people say, "This is Lena's little girl. Isn't it a pity she doesn't look like her mother?" Another remark she never forgot was, "I do hope Lena's little girl hasn't inherited Cousin Edwina's blue lips."

I always thought that my mother was beautiful, but she went through life with the conviction that she was the ugly daughter of a Southern beauty.

Perhaps ideals of beauty then were as different as everything else. Mother said, and she was right: "It just isn't possible for you and the children to understand the social barriers which existed after the war. We were terribly poor, and we bitterly resented the people from the North with money, particularly the carpetbaggers who had made their money getting fat on our defeat. The old Southerners stuck together, and the people from the North and West, who had come after the war, founded their own social group. They could afford more luxuries. They had more freedom."

Freedom from hunger; freedom to buy new clothes in new fashions; freedom from the strict rules of courtesy which were all that was left of the pre-war way of life; and freedom from the rigid religious observances of the old Southerners. Mother never forgot that the Northerners went to theatre and to concerts during Lent, while she had to go to church every day. There was always morning prayer at home for the entire household. Sundays were spent largely at church, and the only game allowed the children was the Bible game, which they all loved, since it was highly competitive, and dealt with the more colorful stories. The Bible was well known by the children, and Mother laughed as she told us that it was their "dirty book." They used to hide in the closet and read the passages the grownups had not read aloud during family prayer.

Not all that they read was understood. One day in Sunday school Mother innocently asked the teacher (a cousin, of course) what a foreskin was, and could not understand why she was disgraced.

She learned her numbers when she was very small, playing cribbage with Ampa and casino with Amma. Up until this summer she has been able to play cribbage and solitaire; last summer she played bridge, although her game was no longer sharp and swift. I've never been any good at cards, but both Hugh and Josephine noticed when her playing began to slip.

Jacksonville when Mother was a little girl had roads mostly of deep sand. Bay Street was paved with round cypress blocks, and a few streets had a kind of shredded palmetto, brown in color, which looked like moss. On some of the larger streets were crushed oyster shells. Even when I was a little girl there were still some shell streets, and the street in front of Dearma's house was made of cypress blocks. That's all changed, now. The swing vines are gone because the great trees they hung from are gone. The wild river banks are lined with houses. But it does not do to look back on that world with too much nostalgia. There was great bitterness and resentment. Mado was one of the few whose spirit was never warped.

A large part of Mother's childhood and young girlhood was spent at the beach. When Mado built the beach cottage there was no way to reach it except by boat, but in the 1890's a narrow-gauge railroad was built from South Jacksonville to San Pablo. Mado's cottage was built piecemeal, with rooms added on as extra grandchildren and a little money were acquired. Mother wrote, "We were in Mado's little cottage at the beach at the time of the Charleston earthquake. I was three years old. Aunt Caro Hallowes was visiting us, and Papa was on one of the Clyde ships on his way home from a business trip in the North.

"The earthquake was so terrible in Charleston that we even felt it at the beach. I was sleeping in a trundle bed, pulled out from under Mado's bed. In her fright, Mama rushed in after me and I remember being picked up in her arms, and she ran with me down the causeway to the beach. It was the worst possible thing she could have done, but thank God there was no tidal wave. Papa said they felt the earthquake on the ship far out at sea. The earthquake wasn't as bad in Savannah as it was in Charleston, but Papa said that when the ship put in at Savannah, people were camping out in the streets, afraid to stay in their houses."

The only road at the beach was the beach itself. The cottage fronted the ocean; from the back veranda one could see a sandy track which barely passed for a road, and then there was a long, wild view across the scrub to the marshes and an occasional oasis of royal palms.

"The train made two trips a day, going to town in the morning and back in the afternoon. The great event of the day was to meet the afternoon train. The tracks were level with the platform, and by crouching down and putting your ear on the rail, you could hear throbbing many minutes before the train came in sight. We children used to take two pins, cross them and lay them on the rails, and after the train had come by and flattened them into a cross, we would retrieve them and put them among our treasures.

"There was a big, covered pavilion at the end of the line, right on the ocean front, with an artesian well and a sort of fountain spouting fresh sulphur water." Anybody who hasn't grown up on sulphur water is apt to find it distasteful; perhaps it does smell like rotten eggs, but to me it is good and healthy, redolent of sun and wind and sea.

My childhood visits to Dearma were much like Mother's to Mado. We got up early and bathed in the ocean. When we wanted crabs, we waded in front of the cottage with a crab net. The people who lived in the scrub brought in vegetables and eggs, and there were plenty of fish, which, with hominy and corn bread, was our main diet.

And there was donax soup. Donax are a tiny, multicolored shellfish which, when boiled, make a broth more delicious than oyster or clam. At low tide they bubbled up out of the sand and were easy to scoop up. There were still plenty of donax when I was a little girl, but when automobiles began to drive on the beach the delicate shells were crushed, and now they are very rare.

When Mother was a little girl, the dunes were higher than those I knew, and she wrote, "The cows made well-defined paths under the tall growth which I could follow for miles. I never remember seeing or hearing a rattlesnake, though I was constantly roaming around under the bushes barefooted. From the moment we arrived at the beach until we left, I don't think I ever had a shoe or stocking on, and my big toes were usually tied up in a rag on account of ground itch. We always wore big palm-leaf hats tied under our chins with a string.

"During the heat of the day we played under a wonderful natural arbor of wild grapevine which grew on top of the stunted yaupon and scrub oak trees. My mother could stand upright under this canopy of vines, and when the little sour grapes were ripe she made wonderful grape jelly from them."

When Mother was older and Grandfather was doing well, many weeks were spent on an old ark of a houseboat called the *Daisy*. My mother has never been one to exaggerate, so I believe her story that they threw the dinner dishes overboard at high tide, and picked them up, washed, at low tide.

The young people in their strange bathing clothes—how did they manage to swim with all that heavy wet serge dragging about them?—used to dive off the deck of the *Daisy* and then, when they wanted to get aboard again, would call for someone to throw down the rope ladder. It was impossible to get up on deck without it. One day Mother felt the need of solitude and went for a swim alone. When she got back to the *Daisy*, no one was in sight, so she paddled about, waiting for someone to come who would lower the ladder for her. Suddenly she sensed a presence near her, looked, and there was a large shark, his white belly already exposed, preparing to strike.

The next thing Mother knew, she was on the deck of the *Daisy.* It was impossible, but terror had given her body a surge of power which enabled her to leap from the water, climb up the side of the high houseboat, and onto the deck. There are many authenticated accounts of such incidents of supernatural power; sometimes it is physical; sometimes it may be psychic or spiritual, and usually we don't even know that we're using this extraordinary reserve until the emergency is over.

My own reserves of power are barely tapped most of the time, though I've seen them released with a surge in an emergency, just as Mother's must have been that time in Fort George inlet, with the house of the African princess and the coquina walls of the slave quarters showing whitely through the thick green of jungle.

In the hours immediately after Bion was born, when the doctors could not stop me from hemorrhaging, I fought with this supranormal strength to live. I know that hate can unleash vast energies, but so can love. Sometimes when more than the usual feeble human love is called for, there comes a surge of loving power to fill the need.

If I frequently use the analogy of the underwater area of our minds, it may be because the ocean is so strong a part of my childhood memories, and of my own personal mythology. If I am away from the ocean for long, I get a visceral longing for it. It was at the ocean that I first went outdoors at night and saw the stars. I must have been very little, but I will never forget being held in someone's arms—Mother's, Father's, Dearma's, someone I loved and trusted enough so that all I remember is being held, and seeing the glory of the night sky over the ocean.

I remember hot summer nights when the necessary mosquito net kept out the breeze; and I remember the light of sun on water moving against ceiling and walls when I woke up in the morning.

Illyria is gone now and, at the time of Father's death, Mado would not have recognized the setting in which her rambling cottage stood. Not only had many of the great dunes eroded, so that the house was perched atop the last of the dune hills, but the vast, empty beach she knew was gone. The house sat in a few acres of cultivated wilderness, fenced in by a wall of lethal Spanish bayonets. Behind it was a road and small cottages and guest houses; on either side was a boardwalk. Illyria was incongruously in the middle of an amusement park, with roller coasters, ferris wheels, bathhouses, cheap hotels, barkers, bingo, honky-tonk. I accepted this without amazement because, since my twelfth year, life had been constant change. I even enjoyed walking along the boardwalk with friends, and I rode the rickety wooden ferris wheel which had been condemned for years. But, as always, the first act of the morning was to walk across the beach into the ocean, facing the sunrise. Then it was possible to forget the boardwalk and the amusement park and be alone with the water. I would check for sharks and undertow and then swim out beyond the breakers and lie on my back in the long, rhythmic swells, water below and around me, sky above—lie there and let my mind, like my body, float free.

Illyria was Father's last home, and I hope that the ocean helped him through those final months. During school holidays we often walked together on the beach, and it was then that I was able to share poetry with him. He was a ruthless critic, but when he was pleased he let me know that, too. He read one poem of mine slowly, several times, then nodded. "That is a poem, a *real* poem."

I told my parents of my moods by playing the piano. The piano at Illyria was an ancient upright; the action was kept workable in the damp air of the beach by means of a light bulb dangling in front of the hammers. There was one finger exercise I had learned in Switzerland called *Storm,* and I used to play it when I was angry, when I could not understand the tension between my parents, or my father's own angers and depressions. I wish Mother had told me then something she told me later: once when Father was at odds with everything, she finally turned to him, "Charles, how can you be this way with me?" He looked at her in complete surprise: "If I can't take my moods out on you, who can I take them out on?"

There is a Schumann sonata which I do not play any more, and hate to hear when it is occasionally played on the radio, because it was such an exorciser of anguish. But there was also Bach. I came home for Christmas having learned a new prelude, and when Father heard me playing it he asked, "Are you using the pedal?" "No, Father." He turned with his delighted smile to my mother. "She's really learning how to play!"

Illyria was not meant for winter use, and my

parents kept it barely warm enough with constant driftwood and fat pine fires, and an inadequate kerosene heater; however, they had come to Illyria from the Alps, and they were used to being cold around the edges all during the winter months.

Sometimes in the winter the house was enclosed in fog, like a pearl in an oyster shell. The amusement park would disappear then, and there was only the rambling old cottage floating like a ship in the vastness of ocean and sky.

I love the hills around Crosswicks, and the tiny, beautiful lake where we swim, but I will always miss Illyria and the beach.

My Oklahoman, land-locked husband, meeting the ocean only recently, on a small Royal Netherlands freighter, responded to it with equal passion, and not a sign of seasickness in very rough waters. At night we would lie out on the tiny deck and watch the stars swing across the sky as the little vessel rolled in wave and wind.

In the ocean is the mysterious country 96 and I sought for with our poppy-flower sandwiches; in the ocean is the undiscovered world I grope for in my stories, and where I am seeking to understand death, especially the death of the mind as we are witnessing it this summer.

9

ONE EVENING last week when it was cool enough for us to need a fire, Hugh and I sat in front of it watching the last logs crumble after the rest of the household had gone to bed, and he remarked that watching the fire gave him somewhat the same sense of proportion and peace as watching the ocean. But it does not do to forget that fire and ocean, out of control, are killers. The ocean ruthlessly capsized the ship in which my L'Engle ancestors were escaping from Santo Domingo. And the great fire of 1901 destroyed the entire city of Jacksonville.

Mother was twenty at the time of the fire. She had gone to spend the day with some cousins. Another cousin came running in and told them that there was a big fire downtown, and they went up onto the Widow's Walk to watch. It was a hot day, with a high wind. Some men on the outskirts of the city had been burning Spanish moss, and the dry moss hanging from the trees caught fire and within seconds was out of control. When Mother and her cousins climbed up onto the roof to watch, nobody realized how totally out of control the flames were.

As they stood gazing at the fire with the aweful fascination with which one watches something terrible which is not really a personal threat, Mother saw the wind pick up a flaming brand, carry it six blocks, and drop it on the house of an uncle and aunt. Within minutes, the house was in flames.

She said a quick goodbye to her cousins and ran home. Grandfather was there and she told him what she had seen. "Papa, the whole town is going to go."

Grandfather paid her the honor of accepting her words without question. Like most selfmade men he was not gullible, was, in fact, highly skeptical of anything he had not proved for himself. But he immediately started the process of evacuation. Mother and Dearma packed china and crystal in buckets. Grandfather and the boys cut the portraits out of the frames, buried what silver they could, put a few small pieces of furniture on the river bank. A few precious books were saved—including the one with Jefferson's signature, which he had given to William Johnson. But most of Grandfather's and Ampa's libraries went up in flames, as did the libraries of the great-uncles at each corner of St. John's Church, and all the books saved by François Philippe.

Every few minutes Mother ran upstairs and out onto the roof to see how close the raging inferno had come. When the next house but one started to flame, they left. The carriage and wagons were packed with all they could hold. Then Grandfather let the riding horses out, took his crop and sent them running in the opposite direction from the fire. Many other animals, crazed with terror, ran straight into the flames, screaming in agony.

By now the wind was sending great clouds of ash which darkened and burned their faces. The searing heat of the approaching flames was almost unendurable. The carriage horses caught the terror and began to bolt, and Mother could hear the crash and shattering as buckets of china fell to the road behind them.

The streets were full of terrified people, black and white, draped in sheets to meet the end of the world, waving flaming torches and crying, "Jedgment Day! Jedgment Day!"

Somehow Grandfather managed to get horses, carriage, wagons, across the river to where they were safe from the flames, found a house which was half built, and there the family spent the night, lying on the unfinished floors.

And so an entire city burned, burned as effectively as from a whole arsenal of bombs, because of a few men trying to get rid of some Spanish moss.

10

FATHER CAME from a very different background. When he and Mother were married, both had a good deal of adapting to do. They were married in Jacksonville, went to the Ponce de León in St. Augustine for a brief honeymoon, and then on to New York, where Father was a newspaper reporter. They had a small apartment in what they later discovered was a red-light district, and they were happy. Father was doing work he did well, covering plays and operas and concerts. In the evening they would dress in evening clothes, very elegantly, and then proceed to take the horse-drawn trolley to the theatre.

Many of their friends were musicians, and Mother practiced the piano several hours a day. They were nodding acquaintances with a very young couple in the next apartment, whose baby carriage was left out in the hall. One day the baby carriage was not there, and it did not reappear, and that was how they learned that the overquiet baby had died. Mother went to offer help and sympathy, and the sad young mother told her shyly that whenever my parents had musical parties, or Mother played for Father in the evenings, she and her husband would take pillows and lie on the floor with their ears to the wall, listening to the music, and this was both their entertainment and their comfort.

The pre-World War I New York was very different from the megalopolis of today; it isn't easy for me to visualize horse-drawn vehicles instead of our noisy buses and taxis and subways, and I get an inkling of how small the city was when I remember Mother saying, "The little park behind the Forty-second Street library was the reservoir for the entire city."

In summer they went to visit Father's family in the big old house near Princeton, New Jersey. It was a beautiful house, with the kitchen wing built well before the Revolution. There were secret staircases, a secret room with peepholes through the eyes of a portrait in the next room. The grounds were dotted with marble statues, and the marble privy in the form of a small Greek temple had been designed by Thomas Jefferson.

Father was the youngest of a large family. My grandmother had had a baby every year with what finally came to be depressing regularity. After the birth of one of the little girls she prayed, "Dear Lord, please let me go two years without having another baby." Two years to the day, she had twins.

Whenever possible the entire family, Father's many sisters with their husbands and children, gathered together. I'm not sure how many of the sisters were alive when Mother first visited the tribe; I knew the families of Aunties May, Ida, Bess, Gertie, Edna, and Eva. They were all tall, blond, blue-eyed Valkyries. The entire family kissed every morning before breakfast, and every night before retiring, a new experience for Mother; indeed, communal breakfast, everybody seated at the same time around an enormous oval table, was most unusual for her. At home in the South, breakfast was set out, English fashion, in covered silver dishes on the sideboard. It was a quiet, essentially private meal.

Not for Father's family.

"Tell me the story about the breakfast when Aunt Ida . . ."

Aunt Ida was one of my favorite aunts, beautiful, with the family blue eyes shading into purple.

One morning at breakfast Ida and Edna had a quarrel; family quarrels around the table were not at all unusual, but this time the quarrel grew so heated that Ida threw a glass of water across the table at Edna. Edna rose, dripping, stalked into the music room, sat down at the piano and played and sang, loudly and nasally, "*Jesus* loves me, this I know . . ."

This scene delights me so much that I've put versions of it into almost every book I've written, and have had, with reluctance, to delete it.

Another incident from that same summer concerns the mahogany stair rail, which curved superbly down three full stories. Mother eyed it wistfully every day, finally could not resist its lure, and slid from top to bottom. She was wearing, according to the fashion of the time, a long skirt and shirtwaist, belted in tightly; and to her horror she discovered that the belt buckle had left a long, deep, very visible scratch the entire length of the banister. "I never told anybody, and I've always felt guilty about it, because I know one of the children must have been blamed."

After my birth, when Mother and Father wanted to travel, during the times he was well enough, I was sent to one of the aunts or off to a summer camp.

But it was, I think, Father's lungs rather than my advent which stopped their more exciting journeys. I think that Father knew, because of his work as a foreign correspondent, that the illusion of the Western world as too civilized ever to have another war was soon to be shattered, so they enjoyed such things as the spontaneous trip to Castle Conway with the bittersweet pleasure which accompanies the realization that an end to such carefree excursions is imminent.

Many of their adventures were actually dangerous. One time while they were staying in Shepheard's Hotel, an Arab sheik took a fancy to Mother. He was as tall as Father, and he wore pale blue robes with a wide red sash. At mealtimes he would appear and stalk into the dining room ahead of them, and terrify Mother by pushing Father aside in order to pull out her chair, and then would stand behind her throughout the meal. He had a dagger in his belt, and he meant business; happily, my hot-tempered father was amused.

During one of Father's assignments, early in their marriage, Mother and Father used to walk out to the pyramids at night and make love. I'm not sure how it was that they learned (I wish I could ask Mother: did I know once? does my memory, too, flag?) that a group of murderous bandits thought this love-making so charming that they watched benevolently, unseen, instead of robbing them and slitting their throats.

Although I have been fortunate in travel, my journeys have been in a more discovered, more restricted, less colorful world. Travel on jet planes is simpler but (unless one is highjacked) less exciting than travel on donkey, camel, ship, train. In Arab countries, where there were long waits for trains, my parents and their associates would spread a steamer rug out on the station platform, sit around it and play halma. Mother learned this game in the South when she was a child, but it is originally an Arab game, and my parents became accustomed to being ringed by Arabs who bet excitedly on the players. Mother was skillful at all such games, and many Arabs went home slightly richer for having bet on her. It was a more innocent pastime than we would expect to find today. Alas.

Father went without Mother, but with another newspaperman with whom he often worked, somewhere deep into South America to do a story on a newly discovered tribe of Indians who had escaped both persecution and influence by the Spanish conquistadors. The two men returned to New York with a number of artifacts, and some jewelry for their wives, including, for the other wife, Mrs. J., some Indian prayer beads, which consisted of a series of silver beads interspersed at regular intervals by red beads, from which hung, on slender silver chains, curved silver moons.

The two men were sent, later, to Cairo to do a story, and took their wives. In the evening they fell into the habit of wandering slowly through the Casbah, to take advantage of the cooler air. Today's youthful world wanderers are no more adventurous than my parents and their friends; the Casbah has never been a particularly safe place for a white non-Moslem.

They found a small coffee house which became their regular stopping place. There they would sit and talk and sip the strong, sweet native coffee. One evening Mrs. J. wore her South American prayer beads, and the proprietor of the coffee shop looked at them in great surprise, and said, "I have some beads just like those."

"That's not possible," Mr. J. said. "These come from deep in the South American jungle, and they are religious beads."

The proprietor went into the darkness of his tiny shop and returned with a sandalwood box. He opened it and gently withdrew from a bed of pale blue cotton a necklace of silver beads interspersed by red beads, from which hung, on slender silver chains, curved silver moons. The only difference between the Arab's necklace and the South American one was that the Arab's necklace had a phallic symbol at the bottom, from which hung silver moons.

My mother wanted it. She wanted it badly. But the shopkeeper was horrified. No, no, it wasn't for sale. It belonged in his family. It, too, was for prayer, to be used with the Koran.

Mother still wanted it and asked to see it every evening. Every evening the proprietor would bring it out and dangle it in front of her, then return it to the bed of pale blue cotton. One evening he let them know that perhaps, after all, he would be willing to sell it, but at an outrageously high price. Father countered with an outrageously low one. Each evening the shopkeeper would come down slightly, and Father would eke up. It soon became apparent that they would have to stay in Cairo indefinitely if the two prices were ever to meet in the middle, and the time of their departure was not far off.

The Arab suggested that they play dice for it.

Father agreed. He won.

Mother gave me the necklace while I was still in college because it is heavy, and it burdened her to wear it. I love it dearly, for all kinds of iconic reasons. That Indians in the South American jungle and highly civilized Arabs should produce an almost identical piece of religious jewelry is a beautiful and exciting thing to me. To use beads with a prayer, Indian or Moslem or Christian, is to enflesh the words, make thought tangible. Unless misused, it is not in the realm of superstition but is an affirmation of creation, of all matter, of *ousia.* I treasure the necklace on all counts. At the moment it is in Tallis's office, waiting to be restrung, and I miss it.

Would Mother remember it, this summer, and the adventure of getting it? I doubt it. How do I reconcile this sedentary old woman with the mother I never knew? someone who rode donkeys across dangerous mountain passes? who could control a balky camel? who watched from a Moslem harem while Father was with the men during a religious ceremony, watched the fervor which set people to walk, unburned, over hot coals, or to lie comfortably on beds of up-pointed nails? A large nail was driven with a hammer completely through a worshipper's skull, but so sophisticated were these religious frenzies that the nail was driven into the head in a way that did not damage the brain. Even knowing that, Mother fainted.

This pre-Madeleine Madeleine is also my mother, and one I have slowly come to know as she has told me about herself.

Her sharing of herself has helped to make me who I am, and yet I have been free to respond to her stories or not to respond; to be fascinated or to be bored. I owe her an enormous debt of gratitude for all the good things she has taught me, for standards to live by, for criteria learned in childhood which are helping me to live through this summer, which is rushing by, no matter how much separate days may sometimes drag.

I do not know what we will do when we reach summer's end.

IV

Summer's End

1

A YEAR OR SO AGO I wrote in my journal, "Only death will give me back my mother."

But I cannot say, "O komm, süsser Tod." Death is not sweet. I want death for my mother, and this is bitter.

But there are sweet and lovely things, too: this is the summer of the great-grandmother, but it is also the summer of two important weddings; the first, Maria and Peter's; tomorrow, Theron and Joan's. Theron, my agent, my little brother: I am full of happiness for and with him. Another happiness is that this is the first wedding ceremony for Alan to perform. He has officiated at several funerals in England, but this is the first wedding.

We've assembled all the retinue possible for Great-grandmother and the babies, so the exodus—for less than twenty-four hours—won't be too hard on them. Bion and the girls reassure us that everything is all right, they can take care of everything, Grandmother and the babies will be fine, everything is under control.

Jo and Alan leave for New York right after lunch; they'll spend some time trying to get their apartment ready for winter; their furniture is to arrive from England imminently. In the evening they are to go to Theron and Joan's for a wedding rehearsal and dinner. Hugh and I are having dinner at Anton's, with Tallis and some other friends.

We leave about three-thirty, taking Cynthia with us. She's going to Rhode Island with her parents in a few days, and we will miss her in the Crosswicks household. On the drive to New York we talk about the future. I have a sense of hollowness in the pit of my stomach. It is obvious that Mother is not physically capable of making the trip back South. All the girls on the retinue will be returning to school or college after Labor Day. Clara, we know, would be willing to help, but she cannot carry the burden alone. Can we get enough other people who will be gentle with Mother? I will have to move back to New York with Hugh in September, when he will no longer be able to spend several days a week in Crosswicks. And the Cathedral Library must be opened. It runs more or less on the academic year, and I am free to be in Crosswicks all summer, but if I am not in the library it is closed, and I cannot leave it untended indefinitely. Can we get enough of a retinue so that Mother can stay in Crosswicks, and come up each weekend ourselves?

We talk, reluctantly, about the possible inevitability of a "home," despite my promise, but we reach no conclusions. It has not yet quite come to that.

We get to New York just in time for me to change quickly to a long dress, and then we go immediately to Anton's. After greeting our friends I say, "I want to call home, please, and see if everything's all right."

"Of course it's all right," Hugh says, a little impatiently. "Relax."

But the feeling that I must call is very strong. Finally he says, "Go ahead, then." I know he thinks I'm foolish not to take a complete break from the Crosswicks household and the summer's burdens, but I go into the bedroom and call, collect. Vicki answers, accepts the call, and instead of chatting, immediately gets Bion.

I say, "Hello, Beau, it's Mum. How's everything?"

He says, "Grandmother died."

"What?"

"Grandmother died, about four this afternoon."

Vicki and Margie were taking her for her walk, with Léna encouraging them. As usual, the old woman balked, said, "I can't," and slumped several times, and they let her sit on the grass and rest, with Léna urging, "Come on, Gracchi, get up, you can do it."

Yesterday and the day before, she walked rather better than usual, but this negative behavior has been regular all summer. When the girls got her to the door they said, "You mustn't fall now, Grandmother, or you'll hurt yourself."

She went in through the screen door with them, said, "I can't go any farther," and dropped in their arms. Not really concerned yet, they called for Bion, and he carried her into her bedroom. While she was still in his arms her breathing faded out and stopped. Later he told us, "Grandmother was alive, and then she was dead. I'm not sure how I knew. I just knew." There was none of the pain she had feared.

Bion put her down on the bed. He was sure she was dead, but he listened for heartbeat and pulse and could find neither. He asked one of the girls to get a hand mirror, to test for breath, and there was none: it was King Lear and Cordelia, rather in reverse. They called for Dr. John and the volunteer fire department, which has the ambulance. As always in a tiny village, news travels quickly, and Quinn, the Congregational minister, came over.

It is selfish of me to want to have been there, and the main thing which has taken away that want is the reports of Bion's quiet strength. Margie said, "I was flustered and panicky at first, but Bion was so steady and cool that he calmed me down."

For my sake, I wish I had not been on the highway when my mother died. But if I had been at home, Bion would not have had this chance to make a leap in growth. I am proud of my son, and, indeed, of all of Great-grandmother's retinue.

It seemed somehow right that the phone call should have been made from Anton's. Hugh went into the living room and told everybody what had happened, and when I returned, arms were open for me. I said, from the heart, "I am only grateful."

Tallis probed, "Are you sure?"

"Yes, I am sure. All I feel is gratitude and joy. I'm going to grieve, and I'm going to cry eventually, but it will be right and proper grief."

Then began the phone calls, the first of what seemed to be, during the next forty-eight hours, hundreds of phone calls. We were able to reach Josephine and Alan at Joan's; Alan got on the phone and I told him. He said, "Jo will want to be with you now. I'll bring her right over." I said, "Can she drive me back up to Crosswicks? It will mean that she'll miss the wedding, but we must get back tonight." It didn't make sense for Hugh to drive me up, and turn around in the morning and drive back again; rehearsal in the afternoon, tapes and rehearsal Friday, and then Monday through Friday, his heaviest schedule all summer. Alan, of course, must stay for the wedding.

He brings Josephine uptown to Anton's. I knew from the brief talk with Bion that the girls had all rallied round him. Not only were Vicki and Margie there, but Janet came over immediately, and then Jane drove the thirty miles between the two homes. I knew that he was surrounded by four loving females, our neighbors were there, ready to help, and the right thing to do at the moment was for Josephine and me to stay and have dinner at Anton's, and then leave for Crosswicks.

Tallis had been planning to drive up the next day with a friend for lunch; this of course would have to be canceled, but he said immediately that he'd come up and do some kind of service, "but I don't believe in repeating the funeral service"—which would be in the South.

I asked, "Would you do a Requiem? There won't be one in Mother's church, and it would make me very happy if you'd do one for her and everybody who took care of her."

That seemed to him, too, to be totally right. Anton asked him, "How are you getting up to Crosswicks?"

And I said, "Anton, would you like to drive him up and be with us?"

"Yes, I would."

Anton is one of the best cooks I know, but I have no idea what we had for dinner that night. Tallis called a car to come pick Josephine and me up and take us to the Cathedral Close, where we park our car.

When Josephine and I are delivered at the Cathedral, we see lights in the Chase apartment, so we run up to tell the Chases what has happened, and Cynthia immediately decides to drive right back up with us and stay as long as she is needed.

We get home a little after midnight. There had been many neighbors and friends dropping by to offer help. The girls are all spending the night. "We don't want to go home tonight," Vicki says. "We want to stay here." So we light a fire and sit together and talk and try to unwind. Léna, disturbed by all the noise and confusion, wakes up and comes downstairs to us. I go out to the Tower to get my night things, for I will move, this night, back to Hugh's and my four-poster. Léna follows me. She points to the couch under the eaves and says, "You won't be needing this any more."

I am taken aback at this example of the perceptivity of a child, a perceptivity which frequently gets blunted as we grow older. Léna, just a month beyond three years, is still responding with the whole of herself, for that spontaneous remark is quicker than reason.

We go back to the living room. Bion looks white and tired, but his expression is relaxed and calm. The only outward sign of how much this death has affected him is that he wants to have the three dogs up in his attic bedroom at night.

He had said on the phone, when I called from Anton's, "Dr. John was practically ecstatic." A lovely thing about all the kids is that they accept Dr. John's relief at Mother's death. No one has a sense of guilt about anything; they all know that they have taken good care of her; they all feel that it was right and proper that her last days should have been with her family in the house she has always loved; they all feel that it was right and proper that she should have died at home, in Bion's arms, and they all feel a sense of accomplishment at having shared in this kind of death which is becoming increasingly rare in our day. So here again I am glad that I was not there: my involvement would have taken away from theirs.

I spend the next two days, it seems, on the phone. I call Dr. John to thank him for everything. There are many people to thank, and many people to be told of this death, which, when it finally came, was unexpected. The phone rings, too; there are calls from all over the country. One friend says, "She was a very great lady. We won't see her like again." I hear similar comments from many people, and from almost everyone: "I'll miss her." Occasionally I find that it is I who must do the consoling. I say to one Southern cousin who loved her, and who used to telephone her every day when she was in Jacksonville, "It's all right, Eddie. It's all right."

I phone one of Mrs. O's daughters, and she immediately says that she will call her mother and have her call me, which is a wise decision. When Mrs. O gets on the phone she is in charge, and telling me what to do, just as she has done all my life.

Right after lunch Bion drives Josephine and me down to the funeral home. While we are gone, the rented hospital bed is taken away, and this is the one thing which really upsets the little girls, who cry, "That's Gracchi's bed! You can't take Gracchi's bed!"

The time in the funeral home is the sour note, and the "home" we go to is one of the best, one of the least smarmy. I do not mind giving all the necessary information for the forms, or making arrangements for flying Mother's body down South; the bad thing is choosing a coffin. I know that I will have to choose a "nice" one, because this is what the family expects, pall or no. But even if I were free to choose a plain, unlined pine box, the undertakers' lobby has managed to have them outlawed, in this state, at least.

The coffins are all expensive and horrible, lined with cozy quilted satins and silks in various pastel colors as though the dead body were going to *feel* the pillow and the padding. We very quickly choose the simplest.

It is all very different from what I would have wanted if I could have had my wishes. It is not my mother, this dead shell, but it housed her for ninety years, and I would honor and weep for it before turning it back to the earth. I have not yet been able to cry, and I know that the tears need to come.

The next day Tallis comes up with Anton for the Requiem. I make an arbitrary decision to limit it just to the people who have helped take care of the great-grandmother, for many cousins, dearly loved cousins, want to come up to Crosswicks if there is going to be a service, because they can't go all the way down South. I make this decision in the state of non-feeling in which I am moving these days, so I'm not sure if it's the right thing, but probably my instinctive no is correct. Tallis would not want it to be a big affair and the immediate Crosswicks group is all that the living room will hold.

Maria and Peter come right up from Philadelphia, and with the girls and the neighbors who have done so much for us and for Grandmother this summer, we are about twenty. That's enough for a house mass in the living room that Mother loved.

❧

This time out of time in the absolute familiarity of the living room is healing and redemptive for me. Tallis uses a chalice which he designed, setting it with stones which had belonged to his mother; this is the first time he has used it. He has us all sit around the living room as we usually do for our home services when there are too many of us for the Tower. And there in the living room is, for me, the Church, an eclectic group, Congregational, Roman Catholic, Jewish, agnostic, Anglican, atheist. The dogs and the babies wander around. Jo and I sit on the little sofa which Mother bought, and where she always sat. The only additions to the Prayer Book service are from the Orthodox liturgy: stark; terrible; glorious.

The most moving moment is when everybody receives the bread and wine, each person spontaneously holding out hands. This is the Church which I affirm, and the mystery by which I live.

Clara has prepared a sumptuous lunch, and she and Mary, our neighbor across the road, have been bringing in meals for the entire household. They have been doing acts of kindness for us for many years. I never thought I would be too tired to cook, but I have been very grateful to have this chore taken care of.

Maria and Peter will stay with the children while Jo and Alan and Bion and I go South for the funeral; Hugh is tied to New York by his television job. I know that I can count on Clara and Mary; Margie and Cynthia and Vicki and Janet and Jane will all be there when needed. I can go South without any sense of being pulled back to Crosswicks. This is the last journey I will make with my mother, and it is a strange one.

When we reach Jacksonville and drive from the airport into town, there is the familiar smell of salt air from the ocean, with a tinge of sulphur from the paper mill. The great wings of the palms droop rustily.

Mother's rooms are full of her presence; and yet they are somehow empty.

It is fearfully hot.

The psalmist cries out his anguish: My sight faileth for very trouble; Lord, I have called daily upon thee, I have stretched forth my hands unto thee. Dost thou show wonders among the dead? or shall the dead rise up again, and praise thee? Shall thy loving-kindness be showed in the grave? or thy faithfulness in destruction? Shall thy wondrous works be known in the dark? and thy righteousness in the land where all things are forgotten?

O God. O God.

To the ancient Hebrew the ultimate hell consisted in being forgotten, erased from the memory of family and tribe, from the memory of God. If God forgets you, it is as though you have never existed. You have no meaning in the ultimate scheme of things. Your life, your being, your *ousia,* is of no value whatsoever. You are a tale told by an idiot; forgotten; annihilated.

I will never forget my mother. I do not think that my children will forget their grandmother. Perhaps the little girls will not remember their great-grandmother with "the vivid image and the very scene" but they are not likely to forget that they knew her, and shared in her last summer. They may absorb some of the things we have told them about Gracchi, so that these stories become part of their *ousia.* But their children? And their children's children?

And what of Greatie? And Mado?

How many people have been born, lived rich, loving lives, laughed and wept, been part of creation, and are now forgotten, unremembered by anybody walking the earth today?

Our memories are, at best, so limited, so finite, that it is impossible for us to envisage an unlimited, infinite memory, the memory of God. It is something I want to believe in: that no atom of creation is ever forgotten by him; always is; cared for; developing; loved.

My memory of Mother, which is the fullest memory of anybody living, is only fragmentary. I would like to believe that the creator I call God still remembers all of my mother, knows and cares for the *ousia* of her, and is still teaching her, and helping her to grow into the self he created her to be, her integrated, whole, redeemed self.

One of the canons of St. John's in Jacksonville comes to the house to talk about arrangements for the funeral, which the dean is very kindly permitting Alan to conduct. The dean is on vacation and offered to return, but he is tired and I do not want to interrupt his rest, and I want Alan to say the final words over the mortal body of my mother.

The young clergyman says that at his cathedral they "like to emphasize the joyful, Resurrection aspect of a funeral," and I find myself saying, probably too passionately, that this is fine as long as the Crucifixion comes first, that we can't have a Resurrection without the Crucifixion. Alan says that the Resurrection is more terrible than the Crucifixion, and this is probably why it is so difficult for us to accept. Certainly neither one is bearable without the other. Right now I am caught between the two.

The young man says that we must use the funeral service in the new, trial liturgy. At least half the people in the church on Monday will be over seventy, brought up in the tradition of Cranmer, on the strong language of the Prayer Book. I do not see why it should be taken away from them at this moment, but the young canon does not understand, so I dutifully look through the new service.

I do not want to hear the usual overfamiliar psalms suggested. From the few permissible ones I choose *Out of the deep have I called unto thee.* The young man then tells me that "we like to sing Easter hymns at our funerals." I tell him that I do not want Easter hymns at my mother's funeral. It is too soon. I am not ready for Easter yet. I have not even had time to weep. He gives me a small list of allowable hymns, and I choose *A mighty fortress is our God.* Strength is what I am looking for, and the courage to hope. I feel frustrated by what seems to me to be, if not the mortuary mentality, at least sentimentality in this attitude toward death.

Then I remember the Requiem in the living room of Crosswicks. The Church was there. And it was in the dining room afterward, when we all shared the food prepared by our neighbors. No sentimentality there. Only the fortifying truth of love.

The funeral is to be Monday. We are all very tired. I am so tired that I am confused. I feel the way an actor does after too many consecutive performances of the same play: telling everybody (and the phone and doorbell have rung constantly) the same things over and over again, until I begin to forget lines, stumble over words. I miss my husband.

Bion is having a rough time with a really wicked headache. He stretches out on the couch in the living room and plays Mother's records, until never again will I hear Rachmaninoff's Second Piano Concerto without remembering this time. We go to Pat's for dinner, and she gives him a going over, and says that the combination of a very red throat, plus heat, plus tension, is enough to give him a clobbering headache. Nevertheless, he keeps going.

In a sense, getting Mother back now is going to be the hardest part of letting her go. We go to the funeral home to make final arrangements.

Again I feel trapped; I am plunged into the same atmosphere of unreality and evasion and sentimentality that I felt in the funeral home in Connecticut. Here in this house of death it is impossible to think about the enormity and magnitude of death and the mystery of my mother's empty body. One of the funeral-home managers takes me into the small parlor where my mother's body is coffined; he bows solemnly and leaves me alone.

I stand and look at the casket. I try to say goodbye, in somewhat the same way that I would put a sentence at the end of a sonnet; but this sonnet was completed a long time ago, and so were my goodbyes. What I am bidding farewell to now is not this remnant of decaying flesh, but the *ousia* of my mother, an *ousia* beyond my comprehension. And I am also saying goodbye to all the bad things of the last years and particularly the last weeks. They, too, are part of the mystery.

When we leave the air-conditioned chill of the funeral home and step out into the brilliant, burning, tropical sunlight, it is like moving out of falsehood into reality.

On Sunday we go downtown to St. John's for the eleven o'clock service. There, where it is not possible for me to cry, I come near to flooding. This is the church where Mother was baptized, confirmed; from where, after the long Lenten services, she went to visit the families of the great-uncles who lived one at each corner; their homes are gone now, were gone when I was baptized here. So is the original church, which burned in the great fire. I know almost nobody in the pews.

I trickle tears during a good deal of the service, but they are quiet, controlled tears.

I do not know how to say goodbye. All I can say, within my heart, is, "I love you, Mother."

Monday. The funeral. I have moved again into that strange, cold, anesthetized place where feelings are frozen. The tears which were brimming on Sunday are no longer there.

The best part of belonging to my enormous Southern family has been their response to Mother's death. I am moved beyond words by the gift of a jar of freshly made donax soup. This delicacy, which was part of all my childhood visits, has become a rarity; there are few donax left; it is a real gift of love.

Many of our closest friends and relatives are away, during the fiercest heat of summer, but there are nevertheless several hundred people in the church, people of all kinds, colors, ages. I feel their love for my mother, and I share in it because I am her child.

It cannot be easy for Alan to take this funeral, but his voice is strong and clear. I listen to the powerful words. Bion is on one side of me; Josephine on the other. Bion takes my hand in his large one and holds it firmly. When we come to *A mighty fortress,* his young baritone is strong and never falters.

We go out to the cemetery. I am moving through a strange, cold place where I do what has to be done, say what has to be said. There are people to be spoken to, thanked. I repeat how grateful I am that Mother died when she did, and that the problem of the old people's home never really had to come up.

This Southern cemetery is familiar to me, not as familiar as to Mother, but still familiar. My grandmother is buried here; my father; my grandfather, in that order. I have been here for the burials of many friends and relatives. When I first came with Mother to bring flowers, to tend flowers, to take away wilted flowers, I was struck by the poignant sight in the family plots of many tiny stones, marking the burial places of infants and small children. I see again the four small stones with dates all within one week—those children dead of an epidemic, nearly all of a family wiped out.

The heat of the sun beats down on us.

The words of the burial service are familiar to me, are part of my roots. One of the undertaker's men gives Alan what seems to be a synthetic clod of dirt to throw on the coffin, and suddenly the master of ceremonies—I don't know what else to call him—comes to me and takes my arm to move me away from the open grave.

None of us expected this. I start to pull away from his unwelcome, uncomforting hand. But Mother, that courteous Southern gentlewoman, would certainly not be pleased if I make a scene here at the cemetery, refuse to leave her grave until the coffin is lowered into the ground and covered with earth. There is symbolic meaning to being with a person you love all the way through to the end; there is validity in waiting while the coffin is let down into the open grave, in honoring someone's mortal frame all the way. This is what I want to do, what I had expected to do, and cannot now, for Mother's sake, do. I go meekly and helplessly with the professional mourner who would take me away; I do not jerk away from his unctuous hand, but let him lead me to the black graveyard car.

I've written three poems to help push me through all this. The words which come out help to assure me that there may be God, after all. Perhaps whenever we have felt his presence for a while he must remove it, and by his absence force us to take the next step.

2

IT IS ANOTHER SUMMER, and much has happened. There has been the strange experience of assimilating Mother's things into our household, into Josephine and Alan's. The portrait Mother loved is in the place of honor in my study, the Morse portrait of my forebears, the two young women in Charleston, one playing the flute, the other the harp.

And yet—when we went for a flying visit down South to see Pat, and drove by the street which led to the river and Mother's home for thirty-seven years, I felt that if we drove down the street and went in, it would all be the same, the portrait in the living room, with the marble coffee table under it, and Mother sitting out on the little porch, watching the clouds over the St. Johns River.

I have not yet cried properly, and perhaps I never will; there has never been the right time or the right place. When I have felt like tears, I have had to hold them back; when it has been possible for me to let go, the tears would not come.

A portrait of Mother, painted when she was four, is now hanging in Crosswicks, and looks amazingly like Charlotte, who looks amazingly like Alan: intermixture and interdependence.

Léna looks at it and says to me, "You don't have a mother now. But you're my mother's mother. Where is your mother?"

The pattern has shifted; we have changed places in the dance. I am no longer anybody's child. I have become the Grandmother. It is going to take a while to get used to this unfamiliar role. It is not so much with my actual grandchildren, Léna and Charlotte, that I feel the difference, but one generation down, with Alan and Josephine; Peter and Maria; Bion. While they called my mother Grandmother, she held the position. Now it has suddenly become mine, and I don't want it, but I will have to accept it, not as matriarchy—our men are all far too dominant for any of us on the distaff side to assume the matriarchal role—but as a change of pattern, the steps of the dance shifting.

The rhythm of the fugue alters; the themes cross and recross. The melody seems unfamiliar to me, but I will learn it.

The children grow in all ways. Their vocabulary advances in leaps and bounds. I am no longer Madden or Gan-mad-len. When they are formal with me, I am Grandmadeleine. Mostly it is Gran. Occasionally Charlotte rushes up to me and flings her arms around me. "Granny, Granny, Granny."

One night I put them to bed, and after all the songs and stories they beg for two last songs. "*Long* ones."

So I start the *Ballad of Barbara Allen*. I have sung only a couple of verses when Charlotte says, her voice quivering slightly, "Gran, you *know* that's a bad one."

"What, Charlotte?"

"You *know* that's a bad one."

Both Barbara Allen and her young man are dead and buried at the end of the ballad; I ask, "Why, Charlotte? Because it's sad?"

"No! Because she didn't love *anybody.*"

Charlotte knows what it is all about. The refusal to love is the only unbearable thing.

Another time, when Josephine and Alan are away, I tell the rest of the family that I'll put the little girls to bed and go to bed early myself and finish reading a manuscript. We've had a very happy evening; the little girls—no longer babies—and I had a long bath hour before dinner; we had a lovely meal, with the menu chosen by the children: chicken salad and peas. I added potato salad and a big green salad. It's warm this evening, so the mostly cold meal was just right.

After dinner the children and I sing songs and tell stories while I get them into their nightgowns, and all is comfortable and familiar and safe and loving. We go into the bathroom to brush teeth and wash faces, and suddenly Léna looks at me and asks, "Grandmadeleine, is it all right?"

Slightly taken aback, in much the same way I was in the Tower when she pointed to the couch and said, "You won't be needing that any more," I answer, "Yes, Léna, it's all right."

"But, Gran, is everything really all right? Really?" It is completely cosmic questioning, coming from a small girl in a white nightgown with a toothbrush in her hand, sensing the unfamiliar surrounding the familiar. It is warm and light in the house, but the greater the radius of light, the wider the perimeter of darkness.

"Yes, Léna," I answer again. I think of Greatie fleeing a burning house as shots spattered the water about the little boat, and years later being rowed down that same river to visit the African princess. I think of Mado, holding a dying Yankee boy in her arms, her love and compassion concentrated wholly on his need, despite her own bereavement. I think of my mother watching her husband cough his lungs out in the cold light of the Alps, and of my father setting his name down on the empty page of the diary for the new year. It was not a tranquil world for my grandchildren's forebears, and it is in the lives of these long-gone men and women that I find the answer to Léna's question. I must answer it for her, looking down at her serious, upturned face, and I can answer truthfully only if I have my feet planted very firmly on rock.

I think of the warmth of the rock at the brook, and that I will never know more than a glimpse of the *ousia* of the small green frog—or of my mother—or of the two little girls—

and this is all right, too.

"Is it *really* all right?" Léna persists.

"Yes, Léna, it is all right."

And the two little girls and I climb into the four-poster bed to sing songs and tell stories.